China Law, Tax & Accounting

Series Editors

Giovanni Pisacane, GWA Law, Tax & Accounting, Shanghai, China

Daniele Zibetti, GWA Law, Tax & Accounting, Shanghai, China

Marta Snaidero, GWA Law, Tax & Accounting, Shanghai, China

This series provides practical overviews, suggestions and advice on the main issues concerning law, tax and accounting in China. Each topic is investigated in depth from a professional point of view, and will, where possible, include the opinions of CPAs and Lawyers. These books provide useful tools for understanding the Chinese law, tax and accounting systems, they are written by professionals, for professionals. Every book in the series includes an appendix with the relevant laws and regulation and, where possible, the main interpretation of the Supreme Court of China.

More information about this series at http://www.springer.com/series/13914

Giovanni Pisacane · Daniele Zibetti

Intellectual Property in China

Springer

Giovanni Pisacane
GWA
Shanghai, China

Daniele Zibetti
GWA
Shanghai, China

ISSN 2365-628X ISSN 2365-6298 (electronic)
China Law, Tax & Accounting
ISBN 978-981-15-4557-3 ISBN 978-981-15-4558-0 (eBook)
https://doi.org/10.1007/978-981-15-4558-0

This Springer imprint is published by the registered company Springer Nature Singapore Pte Ltd.
The registered company address is: 152 Beach Road, #21-01/04 Gateway East, Singapore 189721, Singapore

Introduction

Although patents, trade secrets, trademarks and copyrights are "intangible" by definition and as other "unperceivable assets" as data and know-how, they all lack entirely of any "physical substance" in the digital era they are probably the most valuable assets.

In terms of volume and value of intellectual property, the past two centuries were of an unprecedented growth in human history and undeniably led by the Western countries. However, recently new players particularly Asian countries, are responsible for more and more scientific research and inventions, which were once the almost exclusive domain of the Western world. In this landscape and in the past two decades, China played a pivotal role.

Unsurprisingly the pace of improvements, modifications and amendments to the Chinese legal system, followed the rising speed of China in terms of volume and range including the part pertaining to the intellectual property rights, which are crucial to economic and social development.

Considering the acquired relevance of China in nowadays hyper-connected world and its global economy, we examined the legal system of Intellectual property, the peculiarities of different IP rights, the available tools of protection, also providing some practical comments deriving from the knowledge acquired during our 15-years-long practice in the People's Republic of China assisting foreign companies during their operations, business and investments.

Regarding the specific intellectual property laws and regulations, over the past 40 years, the system underwent a multitude of changes, one leap at the time beginning from the "Open Door" policy to the systemic and structural reforms implemented in order to enter the WTO. It is, therefore, important to understand the recent past and the present of the Chinese intellectual property legal framework.

Most recently the amendments as promulgated between March and April 2019, marked a new spring of intellectual property rights in China. In this context main pieces of legislation pertaining to intellectual property such as Anti-unfair Competition Law, Trademark Law, were further reformed piece by piece, at the same time major reform such as the Foreign Investment Law which encompasses several aspects of the foreign investment within China including protection of their

IP rights, was promulgated. The next year, the long-awaited approval of the newly drafted Patent law is expected to close the circle.

In order to provide a clear understanding of the system and first-hand insight to commercial operators venturing in China, we analysed the constantly evolving legal framework to better guide them in navigate and exploit it the most. In particular, the following pages are focused on foreign operators in China and on the specific developments of the related IP regulation, but providing also domestic applicable framework as a comparison.

This book examines key factors involving administration, exploitation and protection of different intellectual property rights in China, highlighting their scope of application, limits, practical issues, difficulties but also reform and improvements of the related system.

Finally, although there is still a clear disparity in the recognition and protection of intellectual property rights between metropolis and remote and rural areas, the possibilities are far more positive if compared to the past.

Contrary to what is perceived in the West, it seems that following many internal reforms, China is showing great adaptability, even assuming for some limited aspects a leading role worldwide in terms of intellectual property protection. In registering a sensibly positive trend if compared to intellectual property protection in the past decade, further improvements are more than plausible, innovative approach is foreseeable. We are looking forward to witnessing such changes.

We also would like to express our gratitude to our Senior Associate Mr. Filippo Sticconi for his great contribution and effort in assisting us during redaction and editing of the present text, as well as to the entire GWA team, lawyers and consultants that contributed to the revision of the same.

March 2020

Giovanni Pisacane
Daniele Zibetti
Managing Partners—Lawyers
GWA—Greatway Advisory Shanghai
Shanghai, PRC

References

Drafts, Regulations, Opinions and Legal Definitions

- Merriam—Webster law dictionary Online [link: https://www.merriam-webster.com/dictionary].
- National People's Congress official web page [link: http://www.npc.gov.cn/npc/index.shtml].
- China National Intellectual Property Administration official web page [http://www.cnipa.gov.cn/].
- Supreme People's Court official web page [http://www.court.gov.cn/].

Patents

- Patent Law of the People's Republic of China (2009).
- Foreign Investment Law of the People's Republic of China (2019) in force from January 1, 2020.
- Decision of the Standing Committee of the National People's Congress on Several Issues Concerning Litigation Procedures for Cases Involving Patents or Intellectual Property (2018) in force since January 1, 2019.
- Implementing Rules of the Patent Law of People's Republic of China (2009) into effect February 1, 2010.
- Several Regulations of The Supreme Court On The Applicable Law In Issuing Preliminary Injunctions Against Patent Infringement (2001) revised by "SPC Opinion 2015".
- Several Regulations of the Supreme Court on Adjudication of Patent Disputes revised by SPC Opinion (2009) effective since 2010.

- Several Regulations of the Supreme Court on Adjudication of Patent Disputes no. 2, revised by SPC Opinion (2016) effective from March 21, 2016.
- Decision of the Standing Committee of the National People's Congress on Several Issues Concerning Litigation Procedures for Cases Involving Patents or Intellectual Property (2018) in force since January 1, 2019.

Copyright

- Contract Law of the People's Republic of China, 1999.
- Copyright Law of the PRC, amendments DRAFT, 2018.
- Copyright Law of the PRC, presidential decree no. 26, February 02, 2010.
- General Principle of the Civil Law of the PRC, NPC (1987) last amendment 2009.
- Implementing Regulations of the Copyright Law of the PRC, January 30, 2013.
- Internet Copyright Measures 2005.
- Interpretations of the Supreme People's Court Concerning the Application of Laws in the Trial of Civil Disputes over Copyright issued in 2002.
- Measures for the Administrative Protection of Internet Copyright, National Administration of Copyrights, issued in 2005.
- Regulations for the Protection of Computer Software, as amended in 2013.
- Regulations on the Collective Management of Copyright as amended in 2013.
- Rules on Protection of the Right of Communication through Information Networks as amended in 2013.
- SPC and the Supreme People's Procuratorate (SPP) joint judicial interpretation September 2004.
- SPC and the Supreme People's Procuratorate (SPP) joint judicial interpretation, April 2007.
- SPC and the Supreme People's Procuratorate (SPP) joint judicial interpretation January 2010.
- SPC Provisions on Several Issues of Application of Laws in the Trial of Civil Disputes in Relation to Infringement of the Right of Communication through Information Networks promulgated in 2012.

Trademark

- Paris Convention for the Protection of Industrial Property (March 20, 1883; effective July 7, 1884, and amended June 2, 1934 and July 14, 1967 and finally 1979).
- The Madrid Agreement Concerning the International Registration of Marks (1891) signed and revised at Brussels 1900, Washington 1911, The Hague 1925, London 1934, Nice 1957 and Stockholm 1967 and amended in 1979.

- Madrid Agreement related Protocol (1989).
- Nice Agreement on International Classification of Goods and Services (1957) concluded at Nice in 1957, revised at Stockholm in 1967 and at Geneva in 1977, and amended in 1979.
- The Trademark Law of People's Republic of China (1983) revised on 1 July 1993, 27 October 2001, 30 August 2013 and on 23 April 2019, last amendment is effective from 1 November 2019.
- The Trademark Law Implementing regulations (2014) effective from May 1, 2014.
- The Interpretations of the Supreme People's Court on Issues Relating to Jurisdiction and Application of Laws for Trademark Cases following Implementation of the Revised Trademark Law (2014).
- Rules of the Supreme People's Court on Issues Relating to the Hearing of Administrative Cases Involving Granting or Affirming Trademark Rights (2017).
- Several Provisions on Standardising Application for Trademark Registration (2019).

IP Rights Protection and Enforcement in Other Provisions

- Anti-Unfair Competition Law of the People's Republic of China (1993) as revised in 2019.
- Foreign Investment Law of the People's Republic of China (2019) effective from January 1, 2020.
- Regulations of the People's Republic of China on Customs Protection of Intellectual Property Rights (2018 Revision) effective from March 19, 2018.

Contents

Abbreviations

CJV	Contractual Joint Venture Enterprise
CNIPA	China National Intellectual Property Administration
Copyright law	The Copyright Law of People's Republic of China
EJV	Equity Joint Venture Enterprise
FIE	Foreign Invested Enterprise
FIL	Foreign Investment Law
ISPs	Internet Service Providers
JVs	Joint Venture Enterprise(s)
Madrid Agreement	The Madrid Agreement Concerning the International Registration of Marks
NAC	National Administration of Copyright
NCL	Nice International Classification of Goods and Services
NPC	National People's Congress
NPCSC	National People's Congress Standing Committee
NSPs	Network Service Providers
Paris Convention	Paris Convention for the Protection of Industrial Property
Patent law	The Patent Law of People's Republic of China
PRC	People's Republic of China
SPC	Supreme People's Court
SPP	Supreme People's Procuratorate
The Madrid Protocol	The Madrid Agreement Protocol
Trademark Implementing Regulations	The Trademark Law of People's Republic of China Implementing Regulations

Trademark law	The Trademark Law of People's Republic of China
WFOE	Wholly Foreign Enterprise
WIPO	World Intellectual Property Organization
WTO	World Trade Organization

Chapter 1
Evolution of the Intellectual Property Law in China

1.1 Origins

A common assumption is that over China's long history, the intellectual property matter has remained largely unknown until a few decades ago. When as a result of economic reform and accession to the World Trade Organization this subject finally received some consideration.

Although these events have been significant and have impacted changes in the history of intellectual property, this assumption is untrue.

According to some historical findings, in China the first registered trademark was found on pottery dating back to 2698 BC, under the reign of Huang Di (Yellow Emperor), one of the mythical founders of Chinese civilization.

In any case, it should be noted that early stages of intellectual property protection in China were not so different from Western models.

A common driver between Western and Chinese models of intellectual property was the need to place bans on the reproduction of some texts following the spread of movable type printing, that was introduced in China in the 11th century and in Europe in the 15th century.

This allowed the creation of the first stages of copyright protection worldwide.

However, some interpretations state that the intention was not to offer effective protection for publishers and authors, but to exercise control over the orthodox content and circulation of ideas.

In Western juridical tradition the birth of the modern idea of intellectual property dates back to a recent era, the European Enlightenment. When the idea that knowledge was a conquest of mankind rather than the fruit of divine revelation begun.

Mankind had become the new center of the universe and therefore as the legitimate owner of the idea he had shaped. In the 18th century there was an establishment between the concepts of ideas and property.

G. Pisacane and D. Zibetti, *Intellectual Property in China*, China Law, Tax & Accounting,
https://doi.org/10.1007/978-981-15-4558-0_1

It was at this point that a gap between the Chinese and the Western juridical experience started. In Western societies the idea that authors and inventors have the right to be protected for their own creations even against the state emerged. On the other hand, in China, where the state was considered the center of everything, it was believed that the protection of the interests of the state often identified in the strengthening of imperial power or in a Confucian social harmony and had to be asserted before anything else. Therefore, in China, the protection of works of ingenuity assumed their relevance up to the beginning of the 20th century, only if it was aimed towards the interests of the state.

During the final stage of Chinese imperial history, the introduction of a formal system of intellectual property protection was attested.

1.2 Late Empire

After to the defeats suffered during the Opium Wars between the 17th and 19th centuries, China opened its borders to foreign trade transforming the Late Empire era as the period with the greatest Sino-Western interaction on issues related to intellectual property.

At the beginning, the goods traded were opium and raw silk which did not pose problems regarding intellectual property.

With the intensification of trade in the second half of the 19th century, the first problems concerning imitation of products appeared.

Trademarks and foreign trade names were used and imitated without the necessary authorization in order to evade the amount of tax payable to Chinese entities. On the other hand, the use and imitation of foreign property was also used to take advantage of the lenient attitude of Chinese authorities towards foreigners.

Afterwards, imitation became the new underlying logic.

"Borrowing" the already gained fame of foreign product became a very popular trend and the spread of this phenomenon caught the Western countries unprepared.

Western countries that signed the Paris Convention on Industrial Property in 1883 and the Berne Convention on the Protection of Literary and Artistic Works in 1886 apparently forgotten China's non-membership.

While it still partly remains the case, foreign operators often gave up at the beginning, when looking for protection at judicial offices, due to the lack of knowledge on Chinese law and its dynamics.

Emperor Qing Guangxu, with the help of philosopher and politician Kang Youwei, in 1898, tried to react to those events by initiating a reform, called the 100 days' reform. Due to its short duration, during which they tried to dictate a new discipline concerning the importation of technology, printings and inventions, this reform was cut short by Empress Cixi.

Later, after the Boxer Uprising, another popular uprising occurred between 1898 and 1900 due to xenophobic sentiments against foreign missionaries and companies. This uprising was put down by expeditions organized by foreign forces with negotiations regarding intellectual property being put in their core discussion.

The foreign powers began to exert pressure by placing protection of intellectual property at the core of their trade negotiations. The government reacted by signing international trade agreements between 1902 and 1903 with Great Britain, the United States, and Japan. With specific commitments on the matter, forcing the Qing Dynasty to adopt the very first laws expressly dedicated to intellectual property. These laws were not implemented because of the disintegration of the Empire due to corruption, some internal unrest, and the start of semi-colonialism.

1.3 Chinese Republic

The millennial history of the Chinese Empire ended in 1911 with a revolution led by Sun Zhong Shan. On January 1st, 1912, the country was officially proclaimed as the Chinese Republic.

In this period of transition, the reform process slowed down.

The process was further slowed due to foreign powers will to not to give up the privilege of extraterritoriality.

With the emergence of the Chinese nationalist party, Guomindang, the situation changed radically following the aspiration to establish a new legal system based on a formal legal structure. In a few years, the four codes and the Constitution were published. In 1928, China established a law on copyright based off a German example. The law was also filtered through the Japanese law, which marked an important turning point, despite the numerous limits imposed to the protection of artistic and literary works.

Later, in 1930, the Law on Publications was issued which included particularly stringent limits. The Law on Publications forbade the publication of any work that was contrary to the Party or to the "three principles of the people"—nationalism, democracy and the approval of the people.

Trademark law was introduced in 1930 and then in 1935 it was modified. Towards the end of the nationalist republic in 1949, Patent law was issued.

Although the nationalist government was committed to changing the regulatory environment, during its gradual demise, only a few changes were put in practice. The probable factors that affected these results were: inaccessibility of the courts, interference from the authorities, lack of adequately prepared administrative and judiciary staff that could apply and give effect to the new rules, and lastly, the absence of a class of lawyers that were independent from the public administration.

It is thought that this result was also affected by other reasons behind the reforms, which were driven more by an excessive ambition than by a real change in the social fabric.

1.4 Maoist Era

On October 1st, 1949, Mao Zedong proclaimed the People's Republic of China, which opened a new chapter in the history of the country. This new chapter was accompanied by the choice to erase the recent history by repealing the entire regulatory apparatus built by the nationalist party. This apparatus was defined as "an instrument to protect the reactionary power and a weapon to oppress and harass the vast masses of the people".

Communist China's legislation immediately proved to have been openly inspired by the Soviet socialist model. Intellectual property, in particular, became an instrument intended to promote the greatness of the socialist state.

Following the Soviet example China adopted the double track system as part of its new legislation on inventions. This distinguished the certificate which placed rights to ownership of the invention to the head of the state, leaving the inventor with the right to receive only economic compensation. On the other hand, the patent certificate guaranteed the inventor the full rights belonging to the patented invention.

In the 1950s, a new trademark registration system was set up. While authors and publishers were recognized with rights of mere persuasive effectiveness; the first state conference on contents and publications was promoted by the Ministry of Culture and confirmed the firm control over the State. Which shifted the focus on the relationship between publishers and authors and on the patrimonial rights granted to the latter.

At the time, China was experiencing a civil war and national resistance to Japanese aggression.

During this period, the Communist party tried to rebuild the country by promoting the development of technology and production. This was done by calling all of the productive forces of the country (including intellectuals and owners) to contribute, as outlined by the 1954 Constitution. Private ownership of the means of production was allowed and protected, but only in order to realize a society free from the exploitation from person to person.

In the early 1970s, the reform process changed the elementary and temporary regulatory protection of artistic and literary works, brands, and inventions by reducing the degree of protection. The reasoning for these reforms was that it was believed that it would be counterproductive to encourage people engaged in creative and commercial activities since it was seen as common heritage not as part of the concept of private property.

It was declared on October 23rd, 1963, that inventions and improvements in technology were owned by the State and this declaration led the Council of the State to ratify it into law.

In the same year, the main objective of regulations on trademark control was to guarantee quality on the products. The guarantee did not consider the concept of rights, exclusive use, and/or explicit consumer protection.

Unfortunately, even these regulatory interventions were canceled. The Great Cultural Revolution determined an institutional paralysis between 1966 and 1976 which was called the "decade of disorder". This period was characterized by the "abandonment of the law" and was considered a bourgeois instrument hindering the realization of communism.

Intellectuals were targeted specifically and underwent a process of "re-education through work". Millions of these intellectuals were sent to the countryside or arrested.

In this climate, the inventors themselves were reluctant to seek recognition of the ownership of their inventions; the emblematic saying that spread stated: "Is it necessary for a worker to put his name on a steel bar that he produces during his duties? If not, why should a member of the "*intelligentsia*" enjoy the privilege of affixing their name to what they invent?".

1.5 The Reforms' Era

Beginning on the 3rd of June 1980, with the enforcement of the World Intellectual Property Organization (WIPO) Convention, China ratified its main multilateral treaties currently in force concerning intellectual property.

In this context, the first laws of the 1980s on the subject (the 1982 Trademark Law and the 1984 Patent Law) set up a system which had the purpose of reproducing a legal environment familiar to Western entrepreneurs. The Western entrepreneurs were invited to invest in the country within the framework of the "open door" policy.

The two regulations mentioned above, introduced the principle of the right of exclusive exploitation of trademarks and industrial inventions in Chinese law, by providing a registration process that was a precondition of intellectual property protection (according to the principle of first to file).

In particular, the two laws established that the acquisition of the right to the exclusive use of a sign as a trademark and of an invention as a patent was subject to registration at the Trademark and Patent Office at the Patent Office.

The Trademark and Patent Office was subsequently renamed as the State Intellectual Property Office (SIPO). According to this system, the filing date of the application for trademark or patent registration acted as a criterion for resolving the conflict between several applications submitted for the same invention or the same brand.

The introduction of the regime of exclusiveness and the beginning of the adaptation of the Chinese system to the internationally applicable principles. Trademark Law and the Patent Law provided for some application limits and disciplinary rules. The former laws, in the economic context of that time, were still dominated by the planning and public ownership of the means of production.

The years that the two laws on trademarks and patents were issued, were followed by more than a decade of inactivity of the courts and procedures. This led to the beginning of the reconstruction of the judicial system. A "double track" system was introduced which allowed the administrative and judicial proceedings to be used for the protection of intellectual property rights.

The 1990s were then marked by a wave of reforms that invested in the Chinese regulatory landscape by helping to innovate the subject of intellectual property.

These initiatives were facilitated by a more favorable climate towards private economic programs. The 1982 Constitution showed the first signs of openness with the recognition of protection for individual businesses, family businesses, and subsequently the whole private sector of the economy.

1.6 The 1990s

Timetable

1990 Law on Copyright
1999 Law on Contracts
1992 Patent Law
1993 Law on unfair competition—Trademark law

In the 1990s with the approval of the first Copyright Law on September 7th, 1990, a second phase of regulatory development in terms of industrial property began. The approval of the text was tortuous. The preparatory work lasted several years, and twenty different drafts arose before reaching the final text. This law was the result of a long process due to the critical nature of the matter and because of the connections it had with the topics of freedom of expression and thought. In particular, the debate became heavily discussed between those who advocated the adoption of the law and those who preferred to concentrate their interest on the control of media usage.

In Article 1, the law emphasized the objective of disseminating knowledge for the construction of a socialist civilization and the flourishing of a socialist culture and science. The system of protection came to recognize the authors with a series of moral (unlimited) and patrimonial rights (fifty years after author's death).

China also continued its process of accession to international treaties on the subject. In particular, the Madrid Agreement of 14 April 1891 for international registration of trademarks and the Patent Cooperation Treaty were adopted. Meanwhile, in 1992, the bilateral memorandum on industrial property rights between China and the USA was signed (where China undertook to ensure a more complete definition and a more effective protection of these rights). Following the agreement, on September 4th of that same year, the first major revision of the Patent Law was carried out and approved.

The new reformed law, in addition to simplifying the patent application procedure and the re-examination procedure, sanctioned the extension of patent protection to a series of inventions previously not covered, such as chemical, pharmaceutical, and food products.

During the following year, the Patent Cooperation Treaty was also signed. The SIPO was authorized to receive international applications submitted by applicants of other countries involved in the Treaty.

The Trademark Law was reformed again in 1993, this reform extended the scope of protection, including service marks, collective marks, and certification marks. The 1993 reform redefined trademark infringement activities, which were based on the following assumptions: awareness of other registered product trademarks, marketing or imitation of products without relevant authorization.

1993 involved many regulatory interventions and the amending of the penal law, which strengthened the protection of intellectual property. It defined the crime of counterfeiting registered trademarks. Specialized sections were also set up in the People's Courts: the first was the Court on Intellectual Property Rights at the Beijing Intermediate People's Court, after which they spread throughout national territory.

The Unfair Competition Law, released in 1993, was undoubtedly both political and symbolic. It was the first act regarding competition and also aimed to open the market in the new period of economic reform. In particular, this law was often invoked to fill some of the various gaps still existing within Patent Law. For a complete *antitrust* discipline, it would be necessary to wait until 2007, despite its elaboration beginning in 1993.

Finally, the Law on Contracts, which came into force on 1 October 1999, also contained some provisions on intellectual property, particularly regarding technology transfers. It disregarded the expectations of those who assumed that the contracts concerning intellectual property rights were expressly regulated, as it had been foreseen in some preliminary drafts, which revealed gaps and errors that required a more in-depth analysis.

Summarizing, the changes throughout these years regarding the matter, can be described as witnessing the restructuring of the legal system, by the translation of the principles introduced through economic reform, and by the expansion of the protective systems to align them with international standards.

1.7 The New Millennium

An undoubtedly crucial passage was constituted by the entry of the People's Republic of China into the World Trade Organization (WTO) following the adhesion to the TRIPs (Trade-Related Aspects of Intellectual Property Rights) Agreement of November 2001.

The TRIPs Agreement has two points of relevance: (a) it moves from the assumption that the protection of creations through the granting of exclusive rights is in itself a restriction of competition. It has the purpose of protecting and ensuring the competitiveness of the market and includes the goal of liberalizing the international trade; (b) on the basis of the legitimacy acquired as a result of the aforementioned coordination, it has the purpose of granting the holders of intellectual creations with a minimum protection in all the countries adhering to the Agreement. The Patent

Law and the Trademark Act (both amended in 2001) were the immediate translation of the Chinese regulations of the obligations assumed by the government.

1.8 The Roots of a Supposed Idiosyncrasy

In China many difficulties have been found in the affirmation of intellectual property rights, due to various cultural, political, and social factors.

The Confucian thought is considered to be very important putting at its core not the individual (as happens in Western cultures), but the group to which the individual belongs and from which social and moral obligations derive. According to this philosophy, the individual is placed from the beginning within the family group, in which three of the five fundamental relationships are formed (father–son, husband–wife, older brother–younger brother, sovereign–servant, friend–friend).

The remaining social relations descend by analogy and are understood in the broadest sense to be represented by the empire.

Imitation from a Chinese cultural point of view, unlike Western perspective, is conceived to be a tribute to a previous model whose qualities are recognized. A Chinese proverb states that: "stealing a book is an elegant offense." Imitating also means recognizing a common heritage in this sense. Confucius stated not to invent anything but "to pass on without adding anything, placing all faith and love in antiquity." It is also important and necessary to note that in business, authenticity and sincerity were and are important and real values in Chinese culture.

The values "Confucian cause" are shared and contrasted in different realities, such as in Korea and Japan, which boast higher levels of protection of intellectual property. Perhaps the reason for these difficulties are instead explained by the economic importance of the hidden market of piracy and counterfeiting which benefits from a lack of a political-institutional order.

The strong impact of the closure of China to the outside world must be considered retrospectively. This long isolation was dictated firstly by a mistrust towards the foreigners which were seen as a threat and secondly, due to economic self-sufficiency and cultural narcissism caused by self-referentiality.

Consequentially, China has long been excluded from the opportunity to deal with Western legal experience. This comparison began in the 19th century when the empire at the end of its history, as a result of the Opium War defeats, was forced to open new ports for international commercial traffic. Additionally, it was forced to establish official relations with the Western world.

Lastly, the commercial activity was not considered respectable by Chinese people, in fact the society was substantially divided into four classes: the officials, the farmers (who represented the majority of the population), the artisans, and the merchants. Despite this, over time Chinese merchants managed to become influential through guilds and corporations, similar to merchants in Italian cities during Late Middle Ages. Inside these corporations, the first legal norms on the subject (prices, competition, etc.) were born in the form of statutes to regulate the activity of their members. Therefore, the statement regarding a lack of relevance of the merchants as being a cause of the difficulties encountered in establishing an effective protection of intellectual property in China is invalidated.

In conclusion, the most decisive factor is related to a political-economic nature. The tolerance demonstrated at the peripheral level and also by the central authorities themselves have revealed a form of protectionism. This form of protectionism can be represented by the ancient Chinese proverb "the sky is high and the emperor is far", which aimed to support the growth of the local industry.

The difficulties are what led to the elaboration of the intellectual property rights in China to make more recent and evident changes. Recent and profound changes require a more in-depth analysis, going beyond existing shortcomings and defects.

1.9 Current Protection Framework

The current regulatory framework for intellectual property is the result of progressive disintegration of socialist foundations. As a result of 30 years of reforms, the entire Chinese Law of the economy has been affected.

The admission of the People's Republic of China to the World Trade Organization, which raised expectations and fears in China, as well as overseas, was decisive for this change.

Between 2000 and 2002 Chinese authorities, in order to comply with the minimum standards imposed by the TRIPs Agreement to the WTO members, have changed the whole regulatory framework, from copyrights, to trademarks and patents, to geographical names, all the way to integrated electronic circuits.

These reforms allowed a progressive enlargement of property subjected to protection. A more precise definition was given to the property, in addition to specific regulations and introduction of the judicial protection instruments.

Among the obligations resulting from joining the World Trade Organization, the guarantee of judicial control is one of particular importance. It is also an important novelty for the Chinese legal landscape since the right holders are given the possibility to appeal to the court at the end of the administrative procedure. The appeal can check the legitimacy of the Public Administration's acts and the People's Republic of China has pledged to guarantee the transparency of the relative proceeding before the Court.

The Court must be impartial and independent with respects to administrative bodies that have adopted the deeds to be judged.

Furthermore, in the last five years China has speeded up on reforming, modifying and adapting its legal framework.

Final step of this evolution has been started during the spring of 2019 were many new reforms where announced. Starting from the Anti-unfair Competition law, Trademark law and more generally the Foreign Investment law, they were either reformed, voted or promulgated during the same period. Which someone may define as the "spring of intellectual property protection", within the same frame and under the same principles next year will be most probably the turn of the Patent law revision (as will be analysed below the draft is soon to undergone final approval vote). The common goal of the new reforms—of which IP protection is a pillar—is to increase confidence in domestic protection of such rights in order to attract, welcome and sustain more and more foreign investments in China. The single legal framework will be analysed here below.

Chapter 2
Patents

2.1 Definition and Main Characteristics

A "Patent" by definition is a legal certificate of registration, a legal title issued by a State/National administrative body that grant the owner certain rights on its invention. Patents grant an exclusive right on the invention, vested subjects retain the right to prevent others from making, using or selling an invention without their permission.

Similar to Trademarks and opposite to Copyrights (refer to related sections of this publication) Patent rights are acquired through application and after successful obtainment of registration certificate. In order to obtain it, the owner is required to submit the invention to be protected which will undergo administrative examination and finally public disclosure. Notably, granted patent are available in detail on a public database after examination.

Moreover, Patent as many other intellectual property registered rights, enjoys merely national value: its validity and enforceability is limited within national borders of place of registration—if not extended or granted protection by another State within its border in virtue of an international convention or a bilateral agreement.

Therefore, an American or European patent is not automatically recognized in China or elsewhere if no agreement was reached between states, nor is granted automatically in third countries without a specific request of the patentor. In this respect it is important to remind that even when extension of registration is obtainable, there is a time frame. This last aspect it is now of the utmost importance, as in recent years the global competition between companies has increased dramatically, long-term planning in IP protection shall be implemented. To safely navigate the global market, it's important to obtain patents in different countries and perhaps most importantly to plan in advance which portions of the market shall be covered by registration. To plan IP protection plan in advance will help a company to achieve a faster and safer internationalization and expansion in foreign markets, with a more rational use of its own resources.

G. Pisacane and D. Zibetti, *Intellectual Property in China*, China Law, Tax & Accounting,
https://doi.org/10.1007/978-981-15-4558-0_2

For Patents more than for Trademarks, a very broad protection in term of territories is obtainable only requesting a set of different registrations and some extensions to the first. However, the process its rather costly (a global coverage in addition, is difficult to achieve) and not necessarily advisable. In most cases, market players focus on most profitable portion of the market, i.e. USA, Europe, Japan and China. When it comes to pinpoint the most suitable set of registrations there is no one fixed, certain or definitive answer for a given group, type or size of companies. It very much depends on the specific company core business and business plan.

As for PRC, however, in case the company is proprietor of IP rights connected to an innovative invention, utility process or either a design, which is part of the company core business, to safely enter into the Chinese market it is, very advisable if not vital to register relevant IP rights domestically, in the permitted categories.

As it is for Trademarks protection, in People's Republic of China the office called China National Intellectual Property Administration or "CNIPA" (formerly known as SIPO) through an entity called 'Patent Office' manages applications for patent registration: examination, re-examination and invalidation (and renewal). Secondly, the CNIPA also administer its local branches the local patent management bureaus (also known as local intellectual property administrations, local IPAs). Main functions of IPAs are to locally enact regional as well as national policies, promote among local companies the use of patents to protect their innovations and most importantly, surveil on the application of the law and handle the administrative protection of patents whenever required. This administrative protection in China, is granted to patent owners jointly with judicial protection.

2.2 Law and Regulations

As for many other fields of civil and commercial law in China, the legal framework of patent is composed of a main piece of legislation which states general principles—further enriched by rules and regulations issued by several administrative bodies that implement and sensibly specify the very scope of application of the same law. Specifically, for Patents, the Patent law of PRC is sensibly integrated by CNIPA rules and by the Supreme Court Opinions which are issued periodically, and together they constitute the main core of the legal framework.

PRC issued its first Patent law in 1985 together with the related implementing regulations, provisions mostly inspired by other socialist countries. In fact, the first draft as enacted showed strong similarities with the principles contained in the German and Japanese patent laws.

Until today, the Patent law of the PRC had undergone three amendments, lastly in October 2009. This is about to change. From 2020 onward, the fourth amendment is expected to soon enter into force. The related draft for public comment it has already approved by the PRC State Council, and now awaits approval of the National People's Congress Standing Committee.

The enactment of the fourth amendment was previously scheduled in between Q3/Q4 2019 (similar to Trademark law alterations which entered into force from December 1, 2019) but enactment was postponed. Reason of the rescheduled are most likely political, legislative priority was granted to the enactment of the new Foreign Investment Law of the PRC (also to gain momentum during the 'Trade War' negotiations). The new investment law has been published in March and has been effective form January 1, 2020. In the meanwhile, the long-awaited Patent law draft's approval has been officially rescheduled for mid-2020, according to NPC work calendar. Patents, force technology transfer and in general, protection of foreign IP rights in China provisions are diffusely contained in the new FIL. The difference between the present law in force and the forthcoming amendment will be discussed further below.

Pivotal role in shaping the legal framework is played—as in many other cases—by two different State entities, the State Council and the Supreme People's Court. The SC contributed issuing and revising the Implementing rules of the Patent law of People's Republic of China (2009). The SPC issued both broad interpretation as well as rendered key judgment and guiding cases that actively contributed in modeling the state of art of patent protection in China. Hereby we shall recall: Several Regulations of The Supreme Court on The Applicable Law in Issuing Preliminary Injunctions Against Patent Infringement (and related 2015 Opinion revision). The revisions among many modifications to the current regime also removed limitation in maximum amount of liquidated damage for patent's infringement. As well as the Several Regulations of the Supreme Court on Adjudication of Patent Dispute no. 1 and 2 (respectively 2010 and 2016 revision). The quoted opinions, particularly the second, issued in 2016 clarifies in a very useful manner issues related to patent infringement proceedings, non-infringer defense, damage calculation and claim essential construction points.

Recently a brief—yet very relevant—contribution to the patent legal framework has been added by the Standing Committee of the National People's Congress of PRC in 2018. By this decision, in particular cases (examined below) appeal regarding patents, including complex inventions and software and other cases were a higher degree of technical expertise might be required in rendering the related judgment, such appeal shall now be lodged directly to the Supreme People's Court. The "report to higher authority" kind of system is nothing new to China, in other fields was previously introduced, and it has proven a good deterrent against local protectionism as well as ensuring in some delicate matters the higher legal and technical expertise of the country to provide its contribution case by case. A previous implementation of a very similar instrument might be found in appeal mechanism related to enforcement of foreign arbitration awards in PRC (under the New York Convention 1959).

2.3 Patents in PRC: Requirements, Scope of Protection and Validity

The Patent Law of the People's Republic of China establishes that patents can be obtained in three main categories which have different requirements, time validity scope of protection.

Firstly, shall be noted that the mentioned categories retain however common ground regulations and they are all to be considered inventions, as per article 2 Patent law which states "*Inventions referred to in this law shall mean inventions, utility model and designs*". The law distinguishes invention patents, utility patents and designs patents. In this respect, the same article states:

(i) Invention *shall mean a new technological scheme proposed for a product, a process or the improvement thereof.* It shall be noted that "Technological" means that the result of the innovation must be something materially perceivable and, in order to obtain the patent registration, the invention must be novel.

(ii) Utility model *shall mean an applicable and practical new technological scheme proposed for the shape or structure of a product or a combination thereof.*: utility models are, in fact, related to products that can be physically perceived and the "invention" aspects attain not to the product itself yet to the new "utility" gained with the new technological scheme, shape or structure as proposed.

(iii) Design *shall mean a new design proposed for the shape or pattern of a product or a combination thereof and a combination of colors and shape or pattern which is full of aesthetic sense and is suitable for industrial application.*

Notably, while the same work may be patented e.g. as an invention and at the same time could also patented as a design (limitations will be introduced below). Other aspects of the same physical object or company products, finally, may find alternative or either additional protection under different intellectual property laws. Under this circumstances the process and works included in the "design", as well as preparatory sketches and related drawings these processes—jointly or separately—may be very well all considered as "creative works" under Copyright law and therefore, the author it is entitled to the related specific protection. In practice it's advisable to consider these combinations of registrations and claims, to better protect one's product or either, maximize the possibility to obtain a sufficient degree of protection (considering that patent applications, especially for invention—may take time and not necessarily be granted) or enacted to limit and or prevent potential claims form other parties.

Patents are protected by law only for a limited period of time. As reported before, the system provides a different validity time frame for different patent categories: inventions are protected for 20 years, while utility models and designs enjoy protection for 10 years which are calculated from the date of the application.

The current Patent law also permits applicants to jointly apply for a utility model patent and an invention patent, covering the same invention. If the invention patent is granted, the applicant will then be permitted to abandon the utility model patent.

This provision helps to eliminate the current uncertainty over the legality of "double patenting". Under the previous regime, the Patent Office might invalidate one or both patents based on a perception that the patent system was being abused.

2.4 Common Rules for Registration and Appeal System

The present chapter will introduce common rules applicable to Invention, Utility and Design patents. The Patent Law of the People's Republic of China recognizes the so-called "first-to-file system" (similarly as provided for Trademark protection) which means that the first applicant who files a registration will enjoy a priority on rights to be granted with the registration.

Domestic and Foreign entities may both apply to domestic registration. The People's Republic of China is also a member state to the Paris Convention, so foreigners can apply for a patent registration in China through three different ways:

(i) Entrusting a local agent, who files directly an application to the Patent Office;
(ii) By filing an application in another state (signatory of the Paris Convention) and then filing the same application in China within a year (within 6 months if it is a design patent), priority date shall be recognized according to the date of the foreign application;
(iii) By filing an international patent registration application, as permitted by the Patent Cooperation Treaty (PCT), mentioning China among the designated states for which to enforce the application.

Notably, the application to register a patent in China shall be filed in Chinese language.

The patent administrative authorities identified by the State Council, i.e. CNIPA and its Patent Office, are responsible for administration of patent matters nationwide. Patent law impose obligations to the Patent Office to accept and examine patent applications on a unified basis and grant patent rights pursuant to the law. The authorities for administration of patent matters of the People's Governments of provinces, autonomous regions and municipalities directly under the central government are responsible for patent administration matters within their respective administrative regions.

As for requirements, this chapter in setting forth common principles, it also distinguishes inventions patents and utility models (common regime) from design patents. The latter are regulated separately by the same chapter. Inventions and utility models in which patent rights are granted shall possess:

(i) Novelty shall mean that an invention or a utility model *does not fall under the existing technologies* and no organisation or individual has submitted an application to the patent administrative authorities of the State Council for *an identical invention or utility model prior to the date of the patent application*, and record shall be made in the announced patent application documents or promulgated patent documents after the date of the patent application (By law definition, "existing technologies" are technologies well known in the public domain in China or overseas prior to the date of the patent application).

(ii) Creativity shall mean that shall mean that, when compared to the existing technologies, *an invention possesses substantive characteristics which are distinctive* and *relevant improvements*—or a utility model has *substantive characteristics* and *improvements.*

(iii) Practicality shall mean that an invention or a utility model can be manufactured or used and can generate positive effects.

Consequentially, for designs for which patent rights are granted those designs *shall not fall under the existing designs*; and no organisation or individual has submitted an application to the patent administrative authorities of the State Council for an identical design prior to the date of the patent application, and record shall be made in the promulgated patent documents after the date of the patent application. Novelty (as above for inventions/utility models). Furthermore, a design for which rights are granted *when compared to the existing designs* or a combination of characteristics of the existing designs, *shall possess a clear distinction.* And shall not have conflict with the legitimate rights obtained by others prior to the date of the patent application. As for "Existing Technologies" (see above, for invention patents) "Existing designs" refers to designs which are well known in the public domain in China or overseas prior to the date of the patent application. "Well known" status although clarified by judicial interpretation, still remain vague in is scope of application, and might be problematic to be recognized during invalidation process or in administrative and judicial procedures relating to design patens.

Regarding "Novelty" it is provided that where an invention (in its broad term embracing all three categories) for patent application encounters any of the following circumstances within six months before the date of the application, the novelty factor shall not be affected (article 24 Patent law):

(i) the invention was first shown in an international exhibition organised or recognised by the Chinese Government;

(ii) the invention was first published at a stipulated academic or technological conference;

(iii) the contents of the invention were divulged by others without the consent of the applicant.

This principle has two basics functions. Firstly, grant a more rapid development of studies, research and business relations by circulation of inventions, without depriving the same inventors of their rights to patent such inventions (for a certain amount of time). Secondly, in particular point (I) protect international parties from possible pre-emptive actions of third parties that may try to patent invention as shown in PRC. The same phenomenon exists in the field of Trademark, where it is rather common and known as "Trademark Squatting".

The Patent law provides also specific items for which patent shall not be granted.

(i) scientific discovery;
(ii) rules and methods of intellectual activities (note: including calculations, math formulas, measurement standard, etc.);
(iii) diagnosis and treatment methods of illnesses;
(iv) animal and plant varieties (note: but plainly allowed for the related manufacturing methods for products of the above varieties);
(v) substances obtained through nuclear transformation method; and
(vi) a design which has major marking effect on the patterns or colours of graphic print products or a combination of both patterns and colours.

As per application requirements rules are similar for all three categories, yet with some differences in the documentation required for patent design application; mainly pertaining to the different substantial nature of the invention if compared with the other two.

For invention and utility model (article 26) *Documents such as a letter of request, the manual and its summary and a letter of claim*, etc. *shall be submitted to the administrative authority.*

The letter of request shall state:

(i) *the description of the invention or utility model*;
(ii) *the name of the inventor*;
(iii) *the name and address of the applicant and other relevant matters.*

The manual shall provide a clear and complete explanation of the invention or utility model to the extent which can be materialised by technical personnel in the relevant technological field; diagrams shall be attached where necessary. The summary shall include a brief explanation of the technical features of the invention or utility model. The letter of claim shall be based on the manual and shall stipulate the scope of patent protection sought clearly and briefly. Other specifications are provided for particular inventions. For instance, for an invention which relies on genetic resources (recently dramatically increasing in numbers), for completion the applicant shall state the direct source and original source of such genetic resources in the patent application documents; where the applicant is unable to state the original source, the reason shall be stated.

Similarly, for design (article 27) provides that documents such as a letter of request pictures or photographs of the design and a brief explanation of the design (etc.) shall be submitted for a design patent application. The relevant pictures or photographs submitted by the applicant shall clearly show the design of the products in which patent protection is sought. Three-dimensional rendering or 3D pictures or simply four sides photographs are required.

The application shall cover one invention/one utility model, but it may claim maximum two connected invention or utility models (criteria are quite strict, risk of refusal high). The same application may be withdrawn before is granted and may be amended. An applicant may amend his/her patent application documents, provided that the amendments to the patent application documents for an invention and a utility model shall not exceed the scope stated in the original manual and letter of claim, and the amendments to the patent application documents for a design shall not exceed the scope illustrated in the original pictures or photographs.

Whereas the application for an invention is received and is found to be in compliance with the requirements of the law (examined above) the authorities involved in the preliminary examination, shall made an announcement once the period of 18 months from the date of application has expired. Upon request by the applicant such announcement may be—upon authorities' full discretion—made in advance. The requestor will have then to apply for examination. The patent administrative authorities of the State Council may, within three years from the date of patent application for an invention, conduct substantial examination of the application upon request by the applicant at any time; where an applicant failed to request for substantial examination within the stipulated period without a valid reason, the application shall be deemed as withdrawn. The patent administrative authorities of the State Council may, when it deems necessary, conduct substantial examination of a patent application for an invention voluntarily. An applicant for patent for an invention shall, at the time of request for substantial examination, submit the reference materials which are related to the invention before the date of application. Where a patent application for an invention was previously made in a foreign country, the Patent Office may require the applicant to submit within a stipulated period the search materials obtained by the foreign country for examination of the application or examination outcome materials; here once again law states that *where the applicant failed to submit the materials within the stipulated period without a valid reason, the application shall be deemed as withdrawn*.

Following substantial examination, if no reason is found to reject, the Patent office has the obligation to announce the successful application and issue the certificate. Rights are granted and Patent is effective from the date of the announcement. Which normally precedes issuance of physical copy of the certificate.

The patentee shall pay annual fee (in China, fee amounts are on average quite reasonable) from the year which patent is granted (i.e. related announcement is made). Article 44 specify that patent rights shall be terminated if: (1) where the patentee failed to pay annual fee pursuant to the provisions; or (2) where the patentee has declared to renounce on the patented rights. The Patent office (and CNIPA) have the obligation to announce and register early termination of any patent under their jurisdiction.

If a patent application is rejected by the Patent Office, the applicant can request an application re-examination, and the re-examination decision, issued by the Patent Office, may be appealed to the 'Beijing IP Court" for review. Patent Office has also the power to invalidate a patent if it doesn't comply with the Patent Law, and the invalidation decision is subject to judicial review at an administrative proceeding upon request by relevant parties.

Procedure and timing its outlined as follow (by article 41). Where an applicant for patent disagrees with the decision of the Patent office to reject his/her application, he/she may submit a request for review to the Administrative patent review committee, the same shall decide over the matter within three months from the date of receipt of notification and notify the applicant. Where the applicant for patent disagrees with the review decision of the patent review committee, he/she may file a lawsuit with the Beijing IP Court within three months from the date of receipt of notification. It shall be noted that this will trigger a more longer proceedings as regulated by civil procedural law for procedural aspects, special law on IP protection and Patent law and administrative regulation regarding registration regulates substantial matters of the proceedings, and jurisdiction is centralized nationally within a court localized in Beijing—which however will celebrate the proceedings with no procedural difference (including right to appeal) if compared to a standard lawsuit.

In addition, to ensure the highest level of quality in some related delicate matters, since 2019, by decision of the Standing Committee certain appeal procedures regarding specific matters are to be lodged directly to the Supreme People's Court. The Decision specify as follows:

(i) If any party refuses to accept the judgment or ruling of first instance for an intellectual property civil case involving invention patent, utility model patent, new plant variety, integrated circuit layout design, technical secret, computer software or monopoly, which requires more technological expertise, and thus lodges an appeal, the appeal shall be heard by the Supreme People's Court.
(ii) If any party disagrees about the judgment or ruling of first instance for an intellectual property administrative case involving patent, new plant variety, integrated circuit layout design, know-how, computer software or monopoly, which requires more technological expertise, and thus institutes an appeal, the appeal shall be heard by the Supreme People's Court.
(iii) For applications for retrial of or protests against the legally effective judgments, rulings or mediation documents on the aforesaid cases according to law, if the trial supervision procedures are applicable, the Supreme People's Court may hear them itself, or designate a people's court at the lower level for retrial.

In order to ensure the application of the principle stated above, the same Decision provides that the SPC shall report on the effective implementation of this principle by local court to the Standing Committee each year until 2021 (included).

2.5 Patents: Limitations, Patentability, Transfer of Rights and Duration

Regarding the scope of patent two first major limitations are imposed by State or collective interests. Law specify that *where the invention in a patent application involves national security or significant interests and is required to be kept confidential, the matter shall be dealt with pursuant to the relevant provisions of the State*. For the same reason it is stipulated that, inventions which violate the *laws and social ethics or harm public interest*, patent rights shall not be granted (articles 4 and 5 of the Patent Law). This provision might be found in several Western legal systems, and attains to general principle of Patent law, descending from the international convention signed between the states over the matter. Another particular provision states that Patent consequential to illegally obtained or used genetic resources shall not be granted. This particular provision relates also to human rights and bioethics.

In addition to the limitations above which pertains to the nature of the invention itself, other limitations and special provision are provided regarding the subject (inventor) as well as regarding the attribution of right descending from the invention (right to patent). For the invention made while on duty, or manly using material and resources of the employer, general rule assigns the related rights to the employer.

The "Employee invention" is defined by law as "*an invention completed by an employee in the course of performing duties for the employer or completed substantially using the material or technical condition of the employer. The employer shall have the right to apply for patent for an employee invention, upon approval, the employer shall be the patentee.*"

Whereas invention was made by the employee not (a) performing any duty; (b) not using resources and facility of the employer, the inventor or the designer shall retain the right to patent the invention as "non-employee" invention. By judicial interpretation—the requirements set forth by the paragraph above are, at the same time, alternative for considering one invention as "employee invention" while on the contrary, they have to be both absent in case the inventor/designer wishes to apply for a "non-employee patent".

In both cases "employee invention" or "non-employee" inventions however, the same article 6 establishes that whereas an agreement was previously reached between the parties, the agreement shall prevail. The present principle might be found in other laws regulating creative processes involving employer and employee and related IP rights, e.g. the same its present within copyright legal framework.

The Implementing regulations (article 12) clarifies meaning of invention invented "*in the course of performance of duties of the employer*", stating that the same—shall include all inventions created:

(i) in the course of performance of employment duties;
(ii) in the course of performance of duties other than employment duties assigned by the employer; or
(iii) within one year after the retirement or transfer from the original employer or the termination of employment or personnel relationship, which relates to the employment duties undertaken in the original employer or duties distributed by the original employer.

Finally, according to the same article "the employer" includes also temporary workplace. As for the "material and technological conditions" of the employer includes *funds, equipment, parts and raw materials of the employer or technological materials which are not made available to the public*, etc.

Notwithstanding which subject is entitled to patent the invention—the right of receive the remuneration lays with its inventor. In fact the entity that has been granted patent rights shall reward the inventor or designer of an employee invention *upon implementation of the patent for the invention*, shall pay to the inventor/designer a *reasonable remuneration according to the scope of promoted applications and economic benefits received.*

The scope of such determinations is extended to a wider degree by Implementation Rules (cited above) that allows employer and employee to establish in advance such methods by contract. Furthermore, under the current regime, with the only exception provided for by the law of PRC (in particular Contract law, Labor Contract law and Employment law. Fiscal principles and related regulation shall be taken into consideration while drafting) the company may establish policies in advance to ensure enforceability of such agreements. Companies shall set forth and fix these policies in advance, to avoid problem within research and development department related to attribution of patent rights. Alternatively, in absence of such policies or agreement between the parties, the Implementation Rules specify that the entity granted with rights to patent the inventor's invention (or designer's design) bonus and remuneration determined as below. Bonus shall be a fixed amount to be paid only once after invention is made, on the contrary, remuneration shall be paid regularly for all duration of paten validity to the inventor/designer. The current regime is regulated by articles 77 and 78 of the Implementation rules which set forth the following principles.

(a) Bonus: *shall be paid within three months from the date of announcement on patent rights. The bonus for an invention patent shall not be less than RMB 3,000; the bonus for a utility model patent or design patent shall not be less than RMB 1,000. In the event that an invention which is adopted and completed by the employer due to recommendations by the inventor or designer, the organization which has been granted shall pay bonus based on merit.*
(b) Remuneration: *during the validity period of the patent rights and upon implementation of an invention patent, it shall withdraw not less than 2% of the business profits from implementation of the said invention or utility model patent annually or withdraw not less than 0.2% of the business profits from implementation of the said design patent annually as remuneration for the inventor or designer, or refer to the aforesaid percentage to grant the inventor or designer a one-off remuneration; where the organization which has been granted patent rights licenses another organization or individual to implement its patent, it shall withdraw not less than 10% of the royalties collected as remuneration for the inventor or designer.*

Beside the right to receive remuneration the inventor shall retain *the right to be named as the inventor* of his/her invention (even after such action as permanent transfer of right). A different set of rights attaining to reputation and position into the market, pertain to the patentee—who by law *shall have the right to affix patent marking on the patented products or the packaging of such products.*

Considering the above, it shall be noted that while the inventor or the designer is entitled to the related inventor/designer's right, other parties may have rights to patent the related inventions or design, this may be very well decided by an agreement between the party, or again related rights may be transferred by the vested individual to a recipient or finally decided by special rules on attribution (e.g. "employee invention" as above).

Ultimately, more than one person may contribute simultaneously and be vested by a share of the same right and might be considered "co-inventor" or "co-designer" or again may be co-entitled to apply for a patent. Patent law and implementation rules regulates these aspects, firstly, setting a threshold to be considered "inventors" and "designer" explicitly excluding individuals which did not made any substantial "creative contribution"; and secondly, establishing rules on management of multiparty applications. Definition might be found in Article 13 of the Implementation Rules, an inventor or a designer shall mean *a person who has made creative contributions to the substantive characteristics of an invention. During the course of completing an invention, a person who is merely responsible for organizing work or facilitating the materials and technological conditions or engaging in other ancillary work is not the inventor or designer.*

As discussed just above, other rules are regulating multiparty patent applications. They may be simply co-inventors, or in a more complex business scheme inventors and other partners such their investors (for attribution rights—please see the related paragraph above). Where the co-applicants for patent or co-patentees of patent rights have an agreement in exercising rights, such agreement shall prevail. Where there is no agreement, the co-patentees may implement the patent solely or license others to implement the patent through a general licensing scheme; where others are licensed to implement the patent, the royalties collected shall be distributed among the co-patentees. Whereas no agreement is reached (similarly as it is for co-author of copyright) Patent law stipulates that the exercise of co-owned rights to apply for patent or co-owned patent rights shall be consented by all the co-patentees.

After patent is granted—and during all the protected period which correspond to the time frame of the validity of the patent—for any third party in order to use a patent, authorization or license from the patentee, are alternatively to be obtained, or liability of the unlawful user shall arise. Commonly for all inventions (invention, utility models and design) a broad scope of action is prohibited. Specifically, article 11 of the Patent law, regarding infringement states as for invention and utility model—*following the grant of patent rights, unless otherwise stipulated in this Law, no organization or individual shall implement the patent without licensing from the patentee, id est shall not manufacture, use, offer to sell, sell or import such patented products for manufacturing and business purposes, or use the patented method and use, offer to sell, sell or import products obtained directly according to the patented method.* Similarly the same article 11 stipulates for design—*following the grant of patent rights, no organization or individual shall implement the patent without licensing from the patentee, id est shall not manufacture, offer to sell, sell or import the design patented products for manufacturing and/or other business purposes.*

Finally, law specifies that the following circumstances shall not be regarded as infringement of patent rights:

(i) where the patented products or products obtained directly pursuant to the patented method are sold by the patentee or organizations or individuals licensed by the patentee before the use, offer for sale, sale and importation of such products;
(ii) where identical products were manufactured or the same method was used before the date of patent application or where the requisite preparations for manufacturing or use were in place before the date of patent application, and the manufacturing or use continues only within the original scope;
(iii) where the relevant patent is used in the device and equipment of foreign transportation vehicles which temporarily pass through China's territorial land, territorial waters and airspace for the needs of the transportation vehicles according to an agreement entered into between their home country and China or an international treaty participated by both their home country and China or pursuant to the principle of mutual benefits;
(iv) where the relevant patent is used specifically for scientific research and experiment;
(v) and manufacturing, use or importation of patented drugs or patented medical devices for the purpose of providing information required for administrative examination and approval, and manufacturing or importation of patented drugs or patented medical devices specifically for them.

2.6 Design Patents: Distinctive Aspects

As mentioned above, according to Patent law a "Design Patent" concerns a product's shape, pattern or combination thereof, when it produces an aesthetic visual effect that can be applied industrially. Innovative designs are protected if registered (please see above "novelty" and "absolute novelty" requirements) and enjoy a protection of 10 years, same as utility models while inventions are protected for 20 years.

Beside minor differences in application documents required to apply which depend mainly on the specific substantial nature of the design, common rules (as introduced in the chapters above) apply entirely to Design Patents.

Generally (as it is for inventions and utility model) article 5 of the Patent law provides that no patent shall be granted for creation (invention/design) that is contrary to: (a) laws of the state; (b) social morality; (c) detrimental to public interest. These rules are partly present also in the trademark legal framework, no design nor trademark shall e.g. include a national flag (either Chinese or foreign); include racists, discriminatory, religious and/or sexually explicit symbols.

Most of the items that have any aesthetic value can be patented. However, other limits specifically attain to more substantive matters and aspect related to the creations/invention related to design patent applications. To summarize the current rules and judicial interpretations, the following specific subject matters shall not be granted with registration:

(i) any fixed construction, building, bridge or fixed structure which depends on their specific geographic conditions and—most importantly—cannot be rebuilt elsewhere or replicated;
(ii) any product that has not fixed (e.g. randomly animated/variable/influenced by other factors) shape, color or pattern. E.g. a cocktail, sand decoration, water or pyrotechnic visual effects;
(iii) Any component which could sold separately (e.g. umbrella's handle);
(iv) Any product consisting of multiple (great number) or several component parts and the component part is not a product which has any value independently (e.g. a piece of mosaic decoration, plug-in piece of a toy or a puzzle);
(v) Any product which cannot be perceived by the visual sense or the shape, color or pattern is hard to be determined by naked eye (e.g. pieces assembled inside a product);
(vi) Any design that is sought to protect else rather than the product itself in normal conditions;
(vii) Design which the main part is an original shape and/or pattern and/or color of a natural object (e.g. a real sectioned shell, fossilized plant, etc.);
(viii) A creation, work which belongs entirely to the field of fine art (e.g. a painting or a sculpture);
(ix) Any design that consist mainly in common sight geometric(s) shape(s) or pattern(s) in the field or category of product for which the design is to be registered (a square shape figure in the box category, a lamp bulb shape in lamp bulb category, etc.);
(x) The pattern of design is visible only when the device/product is electrified (app or user interface design);

It shall be noted that various of the above cases are however protected by means of copyright such as software and interface point no. (x) and/or fine art point. (viii) or again "brand names" are regulated by trademark law. In other cases enlisted above, protection is completely excluded even by other intellectual property laws either for lack of novelty and/or extensive diffusion in nature or market, e.g. points no. (vii) and (ix), or because potential registration in violation of laws and social norm e.g. discriminatory, national and/or religious symbols.

Furthermore it shall be considered that, for majority of cases not included in the previous list, related rights might overlaps with other intellectual property rights, and whereas the same are also separately registrable (e.g. copyright) full protection might be achieved only with cumulative registrations of the different IP rights involved. Depending on the items and their complexity—where ascetics aspect are the most innovative and/or most crucial to be protected, the objective could achieved with a combined registration of a design patent and/or copyrights but also considering trademark and 3D trademark (A shape or 3D mark, is a three-dimensional trade symbol which identifies or is used in relation with goods—please refer to the related paragraph related to trademark protection in this publication). For complex (normally highly valuable) products, a preventive due diligence and IP strategy shall be outlined to avoid expensive and time-consuming consequences.

The implementation rules outline technicalities required for a design to be registered (the most common were introduced above in a previous chapter of this publication). Regarding general prescriptions law specifies that a brief description of a design shall state the name and uses of the design's products and the design highlights of the design and designate a picture or photograph which best describes the design highlights. Where visual pictures are omitted or the applicant requests for protection of colors, a statement shall be included in the brief description. Where a patent application for design is made for several similar designs of the same product, one of them shall be designated as the basic design in the brief description. A brief description shall not use commercial advertising terms and shall not be used for explanation of product functionalities. Authorities may request samples of product or model of the design to be registered.

The design patent guarantees exclusively protection for the aesthetic characteristics of the product, which means that two identical products, with different functions, can be protected by the same design patent, design might be registered with limitation for a set of products. It's important to emphasize once again that, to obtain protection in China, the design must be new: as mentioned above generally for inventions, novelty means that a certain product has never been disclosed to the public before, anywhere in the world—through the sale, promotion or any other ways—before the application (with exceptions as introduced above, e.g. invention displayed within 6 months in an official and recognized trade fair in PRC, later registered by the same subject).

Absence of "Novelty" or lack and violation of other requirements as enlisted in the chapters above, eventually may lead to rejection of the application or alternatively, invalidation of the registration.

Novelty standards are also vital in term of protection against malicious applications of third parties. The present circumstance is quite diffused in China, and mainly known as "junk patent" similar to "trademark squatting" but with few more implications. Under the current regime—patents are granted without substantive examination, many of the design patents currently existing in China are to be considered as "junk patents", obtained either:

(a) to be used against prior registrant in other country in case he/she may enter the Chinese market; or
(b) as a marketing tool (supposedly) to indicate innovative character of a company.

Notably often such junk patent certificates are displayed in the factory site, hanged on company's HQ walls, or digitalized and posted on websites with the sole purpose of promoting one's company name or image. Last amendment of the law was specifically made also to curb this phenomenon. The "Absolute Novelty" standard as introduced briefly above, was introduced to this end. Last revision of Patent law in 2009 and Implementing regulation 2010 provided that new design must contain "noticeable" differences from pre-existing one. Therefore, a design patent may now be invalidated, if the same or a similar one was sold or publicly displayed anywhere before the filing date. While under old system publication, display and use only account PRC territory, with the last amendment, new tools of protection were introduced: authorities were empowered to better reject "junk applications" and inventors which previously had registered related rights or anyway can prove any previous worldwide use and pre-existence of a given design, may have a better change to invalidate a posthumous granted "junk patent".

For the same reason, to further differentiate among inventions, the reformed Patent law compel now applicants to submit a brief description to their design, which was previously optional (article 27). The description can be used to interpret the design, and the CNIPA shall now reject all the applications which don't comply with the law.

Beside junk application, law regulates also common violations of patented rights. Common infringement of design patents occurs where a design is identical or similar to the patented design used for an identical or similar product. If there is no difference in the overall visual effect, the patented designs will be regarded as "identical." Similarly, where there is no substantial difference in the overall visual effect, the Courts will regard this design and the patented design as "similar." The infringement shall pertain to the exterior appearance and its representation in "the eye of common consumers". However, this principle begs for an unintended consequence, where the components are installed inside a final product, and therefore not visible and/or they add no value to the appearance of the products, they do not constitute any infringement and no claim shall be made against its seller or distributor. This change makes it difficult for patent holders in some industries to enforce their design patents where products are assembled in the interior of products (e.g. mechanical components).

2.7 Licensing and Transfer of Patents

Patent rights of any kind might be assigned freely before the application is made (except for the obligations towards the inventor), subsequently the same rights may be licensed to third parties, as well as, permanently transferred while registration is active.

Attribution and transfer of registration rights were introduced in the previous chapters. As for licensing, the license is a contract which temporarily assign right to exploit the patent and shall be concluded in writing. In addition, article 12 of Patent law specifies that licensee shall pay royalties to the licensor and shall have no right to license to other parties (without consent of the licensor). Generally, as reported above lack of consensus or either license always constitute violation of patented rights or better infringement thereof.

In consideration of the above and bearing in mind that without consent no patent shall be used or implemented, the same protection might prevent innovation or development of certain technologies and/or business. Particularly considering that for technical inventions patent have a validity of 20 years, a system has been enacted to unlock certain fields and boost opportunities for creating and developing innovation which might be beneficial to a plethora of users, sacrificing the full extension of one particular paten holder, under special circumstances, compelling him/her to grant license upon request.

The Patent office of the PRC ranks globally as no. 2 for number of applications, with a tremendous traffic of request made every year. Especially recently where total amount of patent requested—and perhaps more notably also granted—almost double up each year. The problem of having a great amount of applications and more importantly many registrations granting a great number of exclusive rights, especially whenever those are not fully exploited (might be the case of protection patent, or junk patent explained above), may finally impair innovation process, nullify market competition (e.g. monopoly) and/or create potential overlaps (and eventually block new related or similar applications) even "damaging" collective and public interest. To mitigate this specific issue the legal framework, provide that a compulsory licensing may be requested under certain requirement and fixed circumstances and eventually obtained.

Both private and public entities are entitled to request a compulsory license.

Here enlisted main conditions under which compulsory licensing may *eventually* be granted:

(i) Where the patent owner itself has done no insufficient exploitation of the paten, without plausible justification, within 3 years beginning from the date of issuance and within four years from the filling date, upon request to exploit from an entity that has resources to do so; (as a deterrent for junk and protective patents);
(ii) Where the patent owner conduct, in exercising the related patent rights, is to be deemed as "monopoly", for the purpose of eliminating or mitigate the adverse effect of such monopoly on competition, upon request of an entity or an individual with resources to exploit the patent; (to increase competition as a tool of boost innovation);
(iii) Where a later patent reflects major substantive technological breakthrough that is of significant economic value, but its implementation depends on a prior patent, shall be granted upon request of the owner of the new patent to exploit the old patent, or either vice versa upon request of the owner of the old patent to exploit the new patent; (here also innovation and tech development is protected as a common and superior good, but opportunity to exploit is also equally recognized to the prior proprietor of the surpassed technology);
(iv) In a state of emergency or unusual conditions arises for the purpose of public interest;
(v) For the purpose of public health where the patent is a pharmaceutical patent (such as a vaccine or other medical equipment during e.g. virus outbreak);

It shall be noted that compulsory licensing is provided for private business operators in cases no. 1, 2 and 3, while State enterprises are admitted not only but also to no. 4 and 5.

Although these provisions are not newly introduced, it shall be noted that, in practice it is utterly hard to be granted, at least until present times. Nevertheless, the system is fully implementable.

CNIPA shall have jurisdiction over the matter, in case request is granted, royalties must be paid to the Licensor in a reasonable and fair amount, with any disregard of its previous exploitation or non-exploitation of the patented rights. As for general rules explained above, whereas the amounts are not decided jointly in agreement between the parties, law provides a mechanism for evaluation of the same.

Finally, regarding transfer article 10 explicitly provides—as a general rule—that both the rights to apply for patent and patented rights may be transferred. If the transfer involves a domestic company or a domestic individual proposing to transfer the rights to apply for patent or transfer patent rights to a foreign individual, foreign enterprise or any other foreign organization special rules and formalities shall apply, if not respected the transfer will be deemed as invalid. Foreign M&A operations in PRC involving patent of a domestic company shall be carried out accordingly in adherence with the law. Furthermore, no matter whereas domestic or not, the parties concerned shall enter into a contract in writing for transfer of the rights to apply for patent or transfer of patent rights, and process registration formalities with the patent administrative authorities of the State Council, and the patent administrative authorities of the State Council shall make a public announcement. The transfer of the rights to apply for patent or transfer of patent rights shall be effective from the date of registration. Normally transfer include a transfer fee. Special rules apply to patents transfer and subsequent invalidation, we shall emphasize that according to PRC law, an invalidated patent shall be deemed as "nonexistent". On this regard after a patent is declared invalid, article 47 specifies that rights which are declared to be invalid shall be deemed to be non-existent, *a decision on declaring the patent rights to be invalid shall not have retrospective effect on a ruling or written mediation on patent infringement made and enforced by a People's Court before the patent rights were declared to be invalid, a decision on handling patent infringement dispute which has been performed or mandatorily enforced or a licensing contract for patent implementation or a contract for transfer of patent rights which has been performed. However, damages incurred by others as a result of the patentee's malice shall be compensated.*

Where a non-refund of patent infringement compensation, royalties and transfer fee for patent rights pursuant to the provisions of the preceding paragraph is evidently in violation of the principle of fairness, all or part of the sum shall be refunded.

2.8 Enforcement

The protection for an invention or utility model has the specific goal to prevent any other person form making, selling, offering for sale, using or importing a patented product for production or business purposes. Patent infringement, as we discussed above, happens when aspects of a product or process fall within the scope of the claims of a patent.

Therefore, in term of judicial enforcement of an invention or either a design infringement the related claims mostly relay on recitals and scope of the application of the same patent in relation with the actual use implemented by a third party (the defendant in the infringement procedure).

Infringement action can be initiated in competent People's courts (please note that some special provisions apply on specific patent issues, as discussed above in regards of Beijing High Court and IP Courts) or by administrative complaints which my be filed within local Patent Office (or better: local patent management bureaus). However, civil action is generally the first choice for patent enforcement in China, not only because the People's Courts have a full range of remedies, such as injunctions and evidence and asset preservation orders but also because local patent management bureaus have traditionally been limited in technical expertise and resources and tend to prefer to mediate, anyway if no compromise is reached within a set time frame, parties may go to court. Finally, administrative decision may always be appealed in People's Court. Even though a civil claim its being initiated the defendant of such procedure may however apply for a review of the validity of the patent in dispute within the Patent office, de facto initiating a parallel proceeding. In summary, international parties then to skip administrative proceeding for several reason: lack of technical expertise, less resources to investigate and cease infringements, decision as rendered are not final, administrative bodies have similar power in term of injunctions, yet they cannot decide overcompensation. Not to mention local protectionism issue which is more likely to be encountered within local administrative authorities entrusted to enforce actions against the infringer rather than if the same are issued by a Court of law.

Judicial infringement actions have substantially two main functions: (a) cease the violation; (b) seek to obtain compensation and satisfactory damages to be liquidated in favor of the infringed entity. In addition, the Tribunal may order interim measures, which are a very useful tool in enforcing IP rights in China.

Injunctions were introduced in 2001 in order to comply with future accession to the WTO and similarly as it is for copyright (which follows patent regulation), and trademark (that counts in its own set of rules) the same orders may be issued by the Court upon claimant request for two main purposes:

(i) Cease and prevent further infringements—(article 66 Patent law) *where the patentee or stakeholder can show proof to prove that others are implementing or will be implementing an infringement of patent rights, and his/her legitimate rights and interests will suffer from irreparable damages if such infringement or impending infringement is not stopped promptly, the patentee or stakeholder may, prior to filing a lawsuit, apply to a People's Court to adopt measures to order that the relevant acts be stopped.* When there is an error in identifying the target of such measures, or request is dictated by different purpose other than the one enlisted (competition issues with the defendant) article 66 further provide for liability in case of injunction's request abuse, specifically compelling the applicant to compensate "actual losses" to the illegitimate target of such injunction.

(ii) Property and/or Evidence Preservation (as per article 67 of Patent law)—*for the purpose of stopping a patent infringement act and under the circumstances that evidence may be lost or become irrecoverable in the future, the patentee or stakeholder may, prior to filing a lawsuit, apply to a People's Court for preservation of evidence. The People's Court adopting preservation measures may order the applicant to provide guarantee, the applicant does not provide guarantee, the application shall be rejected.* The Court, at its discretion and in consideration of actual circumstances related to matter, shall determine the amount of such security to be paid by the applicant in order to obtain the measure.

In both cases, preliminary injunction and/or preservation measures the Court shall decide within 48 h beginning from the application. The Court shall notify the decision to the applicant within the set period of time, either party has the right to appeal. In any case, the execution of such preliminary injunction is not suspended during revision whereas granted.

On the other hand, the applicant shall start the related procedure within 15 days beginning from the day upon which the measure is granted, if no procedure is commenced within the time frame, the measure shall be revoked. Normally, once issued the interim measure is immediately effective (and executable) and shall remain in effect during the entire procedure. However, Court may also exercise discretion in term of scope of measure, in both range and time frame of duration. In case of disagreement with the decision of the Court, the applicant retains the right to apply for review, as well as for the extension after the injunction expires—also in this case Court shall decide within the timeframe provided by the law.

Evidence preservation carried out jointly with a proper collection of evidence before commencing the procedure are both fundamental in building a successful infringement claim. In fact, considering the principles of Civil Procedure and—more generally the Chinese trial system legal framework—the burden of proof lays on the claimant which has necessarily to prove its allegations of infringement against the defendant. These observations might be obvious for operators used to navigate a civil law system, yet might ingenerate confusion for consultant, lawyers, companies that are more used to a common law system and/or that will evaluate the commencement of a trial considering "discovery of evidence" which is completely absent in China's civil procedure. A proper amount of evidence as collected might be vital also to obtain a satisfactory compensation (these aspects are further discussed below).

The time limit for patentees to file infringement actions is three years from the date the Patentor becomes aware, or should have become aware, of the infringing activity.

Regarding damages, the compensation amount for infringement of patent rights shall be determined according to:

(i) the actual losses suffered by the holder of patent rights due to the infringement; or
(ii) where it is difficult to determine the actual losses, the compensation amount shall be determined according to the gains derived by the infringer from the infringement.
(iii) Where it is difficult to determine the losses of the holder of patent rights or the gains derived by the infringer,
(iv) the compensation amount shall be determined reasonably according to a multiple of the royalties of such patent.

(v) Where it is difficult to determine the losses of the holder of patent rights, the gains derived by the infringer and the royalties of the patent, a People's Court may determine a compensation amount ranging from RMB 10,000 to RMB 1 million according to the type of patent rights, the nature of infringement and the circumstances.

First of all, it shall be noted that this 'multiple stage system' for damage determination with compensation linked to "actual losses" and "illicit gains" or alternatively, possibility to claim statutory damages is echoing in the provisions of all major Intellectual Property law and regulation of PRC, including trademark and Copyright (for a more extensive discussion on issues to prove 'actual losses' and/or 'illicit gains' please see the related chapter in Copyright section). Furthermore, as it will be highlighted in the last paragraph of this chapter, the statutory maximum amount, which is for many reason, often used as the preferred way to determine amount of damages to be liquidated, it has been increased (copyright and trademark infringement) or is planned to be increased (last chapter below, regarding the amendment of the current Patent law).

Secondly, as a rule the compensation amount shall also include the reasonable expenses incurred by the holder of patent rights in the course of stopping the infringement. Although the concept might sound similar to many other jurisdictions, in practice we would like to point out that "reasonable" expenses shall be deemed so by the tribunal in charge of liquidating the amounts. Not necessarily it is comparable to western legal system especially to those of common law. Often expenses as liquidated by the tribunal do not cover the entire amount of actual expenses and legal fees undergone by the party to, especially if a proper evidence collection and investigation has been be carried out, which remains however worthy of for reasons that reflect on higher possibility to obtain a favorable liquidation.

Not every use of any patent constitutes infringement per se, in fact the law provides a limited scope of exceptions that shall however be proved by the defendant in order to prevent the related liability. In this respect, Article 62 provides that: *in a patent infringement dispute where the accused infringer shows proof to prove that his/her technology or design implemented falls under the existing technologies or existing designs, it shall be deemed not to have infringed patent rights.*

Whereas a party is not satisfied with the judgment as rendered, right of appeal is generally recognized (with some limitations and localization of competence exceptions). First instance judgment might be appealed—like common civil judgment in PRC—but with some differences applies also in consideration of the special system for appeal as analyzed above in the first paragraph of the present section. Intermediate local court is generally competent for hearing the matter in first instances (except where a high amount claim is involved, in this case the local High Court shall hear it instead). Appeal will be then heard directly within a special court of the SPC (please see above Chap. 4 of this section). Considering this special "high report" system, no other remedies are provided except for the possibility to apply for "retrial" (special procedure within the Supreme People Court—although quite rare—it may be granted upon fixed condition of serious violations in rendering the previous definitive judgment (as specifically provided by relevant articles of the Civil Procedural Law of PRC).

Finally, serious infringement may involve also criminal liability (in addition to civil liability). Under the Patent law, in the case of someone found to be "passing off" any unpatented product or process as a patented one, he/she will be ordered by the authorities to cease and desist the offensive act, correct it publicly and pay a fine. In presence of a third party's patent passing off, local authorities may confiscate illegal income and impose fines of up to three times the illegal income, or up to RMB 200,000 as statutory amount. In serious cases according to the Criminal Code of PRC, passing off a third party's patent may be punishable with fines and a maximum three years sentence of imprisonment, depending on the actual circumstances of the violation.

2.9 Proposed Amendments

A fourth amendment to the Patent law has been recently proposed. Draft was approved on November 5, 2018, and sent to the NPCSC for review and comments before final validation and promulgation, it establishes modifications relating to the following areas:

(i) Employee service inventions—the proposed amendment clarifies that the rights to service inventions belong to the employer. However, the employer should provide a mechanism for the employee inventor to have a share of the revenue resulting from the invention, a mechanism which may include equity interest, ownership right, option and/or dividend for the employee;
(ii) Patent licensing—the amendment proposes to establish a voluntary licensing system to provide a written statement confirming the patentee's willingness to grant a license to whomever is interested in implementing the patented technology, and to specify details of the royalty payment.
(iii) Service provider liability—the amendment provides that internet service providers (ISP) should delete, block access or disconnect links to infringing products, upon receiving notification of the infringement based on effective ruling.
(iv) Patent term extension—it is proposed to extend the term of design patents to 15 years from the date of application. Moreover, if an innovative drug is seeking to enter into both the Chinese market and into a foreign one, the amendment proposes for it a patent term extension of up to five years. However, in this case, the total patent term should not exceed 14 years from the receipt of market authorization for the drug.
(v) Damages for patent infringements—the proposed amendment intends to reduce the plaintiff's burden of proving damages, where the relevant materials and records are mainly controlled by the defendant infringer. Punitive damages for willful infringement could result in up to a fivefold increase in damages. The

statutory damage is proposed to be increased from CNY 100,000 to 5 million (around USD 15,000 to 750,000).

This last provision falls in line with the newly amended Trademark law and previously reformed Copyright law which both increased maximum statutory damages also in consideration that in practice—no matter which particular IP right is infringed may it be copyrights, patent rights or trademark rights—it has proven difficult obtain high amounts of damage liquidated in Court considering the difficulties that may be encountered in satisfying the criteria for obtaining liquidation of such damages that have to be related to the (a) "actual" losses of the vested individual or (b) illegitimate income of the infringer (for a more extensive comment please refer to the related chapters of this publication).

Chapter 3
Trademark

3.1 Definition

The trademark can be defined as the most distinctive feature of the products of a company. It is a visible sign that carries the specific purpose of identifying the goods and services of a commercial operator, thus enabling consumers to easily distinguish them in the market.

In China—as in several other legal systems—a trademark can be composed of one or more sign such as: words, letters, numbers, three-dimensional shapes, combination of colours, (sounds, from the 2013 reform that erased the requirement of 'visible' signs), or combinations of such signs even of different species. A profound change in 2013 Amendment is that sound mark becomes registrable as long as it is capable to distinguish goods or services of one undertaking or individual from those of others. However, the same amendment still does not permit a smell mark and a single colour to be registered as trademark. Protection is recognized within territorial limit, which may differ according to the system of registration as chosen. To enjoy protection a trademark shall be registered.

The trademark shall meet also the following requirements:

- Be "lawful" intended as "not contrary to law provisions". For instance, in China, the mark must not be identical or similar to the name, or flag of a state or other international organization, it also shall not have discriminatory content against any nationality, nor should be an exaggerated or deceptive in regards of product characteristics (e.g. "Unbreakable crystal glass");
- Have a "distinctive character", which means that it must be easily distinguishable and able to identify the products and services belonging to it.
- "new", according to the "Novelty" requirement a mark must be available for registration, or currently not registered to be protected.

Search on novelty can be made also in the official database, where the to-be-registered mark shall not exist nor be found. The same database is useful to administer

G. Pisacane and D. Zibetti, *Intellectual Property in China*, China Law, Tax & Accounting,
https://doi.org/10.1007/978-981-15-4558-0_3

and check on status of registration, possible conflicts, surveil on any eventual malicious registration and represent a useful tool to manage trademark rights protection and IP rights expansion of a company in the market.

In China, the "CNIPA" is responsible to administer such database—which can be used to search for existing registered trademarks. Similar to the "EUIPO" (European Union Intellectual Property Office) database system, the Chinese domestic trademark database includes information of approvals, renewals, and registration application, transfer of ownership, cancellation and expiration for all registered trademarks.

From 2018 following an administrative reorganization, the CNIPA oversees both the so-called "TMO" Trademark Office and the body that is in the process of reviewing the decisions of the first, namely the Trademark Review & Adjudication Board "TRAB".

The registration of a trademark allows the registrant to protect its mark distinctive characters within a given market. Although not mandatory registration of company marks it is a fundamental step to navigate Chinese market, as well as a very important tool for attracting new consumers. Furthermore, it shall be noted that, contrary to Copyright registration, protection of the mark may be invoked only upon registration in the same territory.

China adopts the so-called first-to-file system: this means that one operator cannot obtain the protection in China of its commercial trademark in the event that a similar trademark has already been registered by a third party. Therefore it is essential to apply for trademark registration in China, as soon as possible, before entering Chinese market, in order to avoid or decrease the risk that, after one mark is used in the territory, it will be maliciously registered by other individuals in order to sell products, or simply to sell it back to its rightful owners (activity known as "trademark squatting") or simply that other legitimate registrations will impede to register one's trademark. Trademark squatting is not only capable of obstruct certain transaction and affect sales of one company in a given territory but could irreparably damage the reputation created around that product or brand in China as well as in related markets. For instance, if a given company is manufacturing high-tech components for which is globally renown of, one might consider the damage that this company will suffer if the sale of low-quality, or defective components in China could be carried out freely in that market, under a similar to or identical mark registered by a third party.

Therefore, a prompt or preventive registration is recommended for at least two reasons:

- The Registration process can take more than 12 months to be completed and in China the protection is recognized only once the registration is completed; deferring may result in overlapping situations with third party registrations of similar or worst identical marks.
- The trademark registered in China can be used not only to protect sales in the domestic market, but also enforced for all goods transiting in and out China (see also Custom Protection in this publication); this opportunity shall be carefully assessed in advance, even when the expansion plan is concentrated primarily, or exclusively, in the neighbouring territories, or connected to the same.

In order to tamper with issues related to malicious registrations and reduce problems as introduced above law was amended accordingly. November 1, 2019 the new Trademark law amendments entered into force and are expected to play a key role in protecting commercial operators in these aspects. The new law states that malicious application shall be automatically rejected by the authorities in charge of registration whereas the intent of "non-use" is foreseeable. On this respect the Article 4 of the new Trademark law states clearly: "bad-faith registration made with the intent of not using the trademark must be rejected." Further implications and extensions of the principle will be discussed in the following paragraphs. For now, we can state that compare to before, it is easier to counteract and take actions against malicious registration.

Although as reported protection has been sensibly increased the need of a prompt registration remains. In fact, the newly recognized protection pertains only cases of clear abuse in the submission of registration requests—whose damaged individuals are now more protected during proceedings and after the conclusion of the same. To avoid any overlap with other legitimate registrations and in consideration of the peculiarities of the 'first to file' system, it is still very advisable to register as soon as possible.

In addition to the internal system, China is a member of the Paris Convention and the World Trade Organization (WTO). The integrated legal framework allows foreign companies to extend registrations obtained abroad under certain circumstances. For instance, European companies that filed an application for registration in Europe, can claim the date of the first filing, the so-called "priority date" and extend the same registration in China.

In this prospective shall be noted that International system and domestic system in China coexist. Therefore, a foreign company that recently (within 6 months) registered a trademark in Europe and wishes to register in China has at least two choices—extend the previous registration or apply domestically. Both opportunities will be analyzed below.

3.2 Laws and Regulations

Trademarks protection in China is shaped by both international law as treaties and conventions ratified by China, as well as by domestic law and regulation. The first compartment is mainly composed of three pillars:

I. the "Convention on Protection of Industrial Property" ("Paris Convention") As renown the ancient convention regulates many aspects connected (not only but also) with Trademark, as well as with Patents and other IP rights. Among many principles it introduces the principle of "equal national treatment". The Convention provides that, as regards the protection of industrial property, each Contracting State must grant the same protection to nationals of other Contracting States that it grants to its own nationals. Nationals of non-Contracting

States are also entitled to national treatment under the Convention if they are domiciled or have a real and effective industrial or commercial establishment in a Contracting State. As well as "the right of priority" which for trademark is 6 months beginning from the first registration for any other registration to be filled within the time frame in states which have ratified the Convention. The same convention compels the signatory State also to recognize protection to "Well-known" Trademarks, China ratified the Paris convention in 1985.

II. the "Madrid Agreement for the International Registration of Marks" and related "Protocol" concluded in 1989. The "Madrid Agreement" and the "Madrid Protocol" implements a system for international registration (also compared with domestic registration below). Under the present system which China ratified in 1989, an application for international registration (international application) may be filed by a natural person or legal entity having a connection—through establishment, domicile or nationality—with a Contracting Party to the Agreement or the Protocol. A mark may be the subject of an international application only if it has already been registered with the trademark office of the Contracting Party with which the applicant has the necessary connections (named "the office of origin"). However, the international application may be based simply on an application for registration filed with the office of origin. An international application must be presented to the International Bureau of WIPO through the intermediary of the office of origin. In China, the designated authority is CNIPA for international registration from Mainland. If the registration is extended from abroad to China, each State designated its own office of origin.

III. the "Nice International Classification of Goods and Services" unifies the identification of marks in standardized categories for all members of the Convention. It is open for ratification for States member of the Paris Convention (above). In China was ratified in 1988, some distinction still applies in term of subcategories which are a peculiarity of the Chinese system, further examined below.

As per domestic regulation, the backbone is represented by the Trademark law of the PRC (last amendment 2019) regulates trademark requirements, main characteristics, registration procedure, transfer and licensing, as well as infringement and enforcement of the same by providing principle further specified by the related Implementing Regulations issued (2014). Furthermore, the discipline is integrated several interpretations by the Supreme People's Court among those: Supreme People's Court's Interpretations on Several Issues Concerning the Application of Law to the Adjudication of Civil Disputes Cases In Which Protection of Famous Trademarks is Involved; as well as rules, such as Rules of the Supreme People's Court on Issues Relating to the Hearing of Administrative Cases Involving Granting or Affirming Trademark Rights (2017). Finally, administrative bodies also contributed to clarifying certain practical aspects, for instance with the Several Provisions on Standardising Application for Trademark Registration of the State Administration for Industry and Commerce.

3.3 Trademark Requirements and Characteristics

To be protected, a mark shall be registered as provided by the law, here follows a summary of the main subjective and objective requirements.

Subjects entitled to registration are identified by Article 4 of the Trademark law. *Natural persons, legal persons or any other organizations that need to obtain exclusive rights to use trademark for their commodities or services in the course of their manufacturing and business activities shall apply to a trademark bureau for trademark registration.* The following article specifies that two or more natural persons, legal persons or any other organisations may jointly apply to a trademark bureau for registration of the same trademark to jointly enjoy and exercise exclusive rights to use the said trademark. Foreigner—as previously introduced—are entitled to either extend a prior registration (within the provided time frame) as well as, to apply under the same requirement established for domestic entities and individuals to domestic registration (limitations and opportunity will further be discussed in the next chapter).

In general, any mark which can differentiate the commodities of a natural person, legal person or any other organisation with the commodities of others, including text, graphics, alphabets, numbers, 3D mark, colour combination and sound, etc., and a combination of the aforesaid elements, may be registered as a trademark.

In order to be registered, a trademark shall possess distinctive characteristics to facilitate identification, and shall not conflict with prior legitimate rights obtained by others.

In consideration of their content some marks are barred from registration by mandatory provisions some are generic provisions that exclude marks from registration in consideration of their lack of salient features or low distinctiveness (full list at Article 11) other provisions enlist some specific contents which the use as trademark is forbidden by law and an eventual application to be rejected, according to Article 10 none of the following marks shall be registered:

(i) a mark identical or similar to the country name, national flag, national emblem, national anthem, military flag, military emblem, military anthem, military medal, etc. of the People's Republic of China, and a mark identical to the name and logo of Central government agencies, name of the specific location where it is located or name or figure of landmark building;
(ii) a mark identical or similar to the country name, national flag, national emblem, military flag of a foreign country, except with the consent of the said government;
(iii) a mark identical or similar to the name, flag, emblem of an international intergovernmental organisation, except with the consent of the said organisation or where the public is unlikely to be misled;
(iv) a mark identical or similar to an official logo or hallmark which indicates control or assurance, except where duly authorised;
(v) a mark identical or similar to the name or logo of "red cross", "red crescent";
(vi) a mark which is racially discriminatory;

(vii) a mark which is deceptive, easy to cause the public to be misled over the characteristics such as quality

or place of origin of commodities; or

(viii) a mark which is detrimental to socialist morals or has any other adverse impact.
(ix) Geographical names of administrative regions of county level and above or overseas geographical names well known by the public shall not be used as trademarks, except where a geographical name has any other meaning or where it is an integral part of a collective trademark or certification mark; trademarks bearing a geographical name which have been registered shall continue to be valid.

Some special requirements are set forth by the legal framework, in consideration of the specific nature of the mark to be registered. As it is for instance for colour combination and three dimensional or sound marks. Common ground to be granted registration among these three different categories is most certainly, their capability of distinguishing the said product for which the mark is registered among the others. The distinctiveness of such mark is mainly achievable throughout long-term use, which implies in practice hard chances to be recognized by Trademark office for both domestic and foreign applicant. In addition, it shall be noted that "long-term use" by definition is not immediately obtainable, especially for foreigners, considering that the evaluation of such requirement (as it is also for most of the criteria) it is performed taking into account exclusively the domestic market.

For "colour" and "colour-combination" marks for instance, colours that are the natural colours of the specified goods are not registrable and generally, colour-combination marks can only acquire distinctiveness through long-term use. In practice such requirement is quite hard to prove and mostly reserved for big-size corporation and their product as commercialized to the masses for a long amount time (e.g. one particular red and white combination commercialized for canned beverage packaging by a famous American soda company, might be registered as colour combination mark in beverage and canned beverage goods but yet refuted for cars) or very distinguishable colour which is not necessarily natural colour of the specific good, well distributed in the market for a long time as one very specific red colour for high speed cars, may be granted in the relevant category but most likely refuted if registered for umbrellas. Distinguishability may be also declared in Court especially if a procedure of extensions of an international registration firstly denied is then appealed in Court. It has to be admitted that although difficulties remain, recently the chances are increasing in a positive trend also for foreigners. Courts holds the major rate for recognition of such untraditional trademarks. However the procedure might be very long and significantly expensive in term of monetary resources and time consuming. On the topic, a famous French shoe brand that sells well known "red-soled shoes" obtained such recognition by the High Court of Beijing in 2013, allowing the extension to China of an international application, worth to be noted that the original application covered "woman shoes" yet it has been locally granted in China by the Court of Beijing only for "high-hells women shoes".

For the same reasons, special requirements are provided for 3D marks registrability. Three-dimensional marks are not registrable whereas consist exclusively of the shape of the goods that results from the nature of the goods themselves/or that is necessary to obtain a technical result. Furthermore, are not registrable those that consist exclusively of the shape that gives substantial value to the goods/or either consist exclusively of a shape that lacks distinctiveness. Other limitations are set forth by judicial interpretation, Courts provides that 3D marks have to contribute to distinguish one product and are to be used as a mark, in commercial, sales, promotion in order to enjoy related protection.

Same as colour combined and three-dimensional marks, Sound marks are registrable in China, since the prior-last amendment of the Trademark law 2013, that paved the way to registrability of non-conventional marks. The sound must be described through numbered musical notations or on a musical stave, together with a textual description of the same sounds. Some sounds are barred from registration, such as sounds that are very similar to China's national anthem or military songs. To be registrable a sound mark (by judicial interpretation) shall have "acquired distinctiveness" it is still not crystal clear what are the standard required for accepting sound marks on a prima-facie examination by the Trademark Office. In order for a sound mark to be registered as a trademark, the sound mark should be not only capable of distinguishing trade origin but should not also be functional in relation of the goods to be protected. In practice, as noted before for other unconventional trademarks sound marks generally may acquire distinctiveness throughout long-term use (please see above for implications).

Other applications of marks of a legitimate content are also barred in consideration of the purpose of their registration. On this regard, the same Article 4 TML states: *Any application for trademark registration that is malicious and is not filed for the purpose of use shall be rejected.* This last part of article four was introduced in order to dissuade malicious application, which before may be freely registered and only opposed later on during the procedure (please see below, relevant chapters). In term of purpose of registration, the law further provides that each application for registration and use of trademarks shall comply with the *principles of honesty and trustworthiness*.

Formal registration not only protect Trademark owner, but it constitutes also a way to regularize and limit the use of a given mark that may influence third parties—as the consumer of goods bearing such marks. On this regard the law specifies that *trademark users (to be read "active users") shall be responsible for the quality of the commodities* as commercialized to the consumer of goods. The same article also establishes certain obligation of surveillance of subject entitled to the administration of such trademark including the local levels (last paragraph of Article 7 TML) law reads *All levels of administration for industry and commerce shall curb consumer fraud activities through trademark administration.*

In a broader perspective, authorities supervise the circulation of trademark within the market, as well as permanent and temporary assignment and employment of their rights. Therefore, any event related to right to use and/or change of ownership as to be reported to the Trademark Office. An application shall be submitted, in the event of change of name or address of the registrant or change in any other registration matters of a registered trademark.

Regarding transferability of rights, trademark may be either permanently transferred or temporarily licensed.

In the case of transfer of registered trademark, the transferor and the transferee shall enter into a transfer agreement, and jointly submit an application to the trademark bureau. The transferee shall ensure the quality of the commodities on which the said registered trademark is used.

In the case of transfer of registered trademark, any similar trademark registered by the trademark registrant for the same type of commodities, or any identical or similar trademark for similar commodities shall be transferred together. Transfers which may easily cause confusion, or any other adverse impact shall not be approved by the trademark bureau, the applicant shall be notified in writing and the reason shall be stated.

Upon approval of transfer of a registered trademark, the transfer shall be published on the official registry. It is important to underline that in case of transfer, the same will have full effect after approval and publication on the official gazette.

Regarding trademark license were, contrary to transfer, ownership remain upon the licensor, the same shall supervise the quality of commodities on which the said registered trademark is used by the licensee. The licensee shall ensure the quality of commodities on which the said registered trademark is used. For licensed use of a registered trademark, the name of the licensee and the place of origin of the commodities shall be stated on the commodities on which the said registered trademark is used. In case of licensing the Licensor shall proceed with administrative duty of registrations within the trademark bureau.

3.4 Domestic and International Registration

As previously introduced, trademark registration in China can be obtained either through the domestic procedure or by the international filing process.

For Domestic registration, foreign individuals and foreign companies (with no habitual residence or established presence) are required by law to submit their applications through a local agent. The process begins with the filing of the application, multi-class applications are allowed, i.e. multiple classes of goods and/or services for which relative protection is requested, identified according to the unified classification system (NCL) set forth by the Nice convention (as above).

The CNIPA is required by law to render a decision regarding the application (which may involve registration and/or partial or total refusal) within nine months from the request. In case of a positive response by CNIPA, the same will proceed with publication of the new mark. In practice, the examination is carried out mostly on formal aspects—manly focusing on compliance with requirements set forth by the law, more than a detailed examination on possible conflicts with other existent marks or to actual entitlement to register and good faith of the applicant.

Further exceptions on these latter aspects may be raised by individuals and companies which have registered any similar mark or have any related conflicting interest, within 3 months after publication. This time frame constitutes the opposition period. Once the opposition period is expired, and no claim has been raised, the mark is successfully registered. From this moment forward registrant will enjoy full protection within the scope of registration, as recognized under the law. To clarify, no enforcement is granted against violations before publication.

On the other hand, the international registration is allowed through the system established by the World Intellectual Property Organization ("WIPO") as set forth by the Madrid Protocol, of which China is a signatory party. According to the Madrid Protocol, after receiving the application, WIPO conducts a formal regularity review and extends trademark protection to all countries specified in the application.

However, in each country where the extension is requested, the application still have to undergo a reduced review process carried out by the selected country competent trademark office before the international registration can be domestically finalized (for China as reported above, authority entitled to handle trademark registration is CNIPA). If no claim is raised by the competent office, trademark shall be registered within nine months from WIPO's notification.

Having introduced both procedures we shall note that, although at first glance the international registration seems more suitable for each and any foreign company approaching China as a secondary market, before choosing between the domestic and international procedure each company shall evaluate rationally. In order to better explain here follows a brief comparison.

Firstly, they both have a validity of 10 years, both renewable—at registrant's will upon his/her request. For what concerns language, within the national procedure the application must be in Chinese. Furthermore, as reported above, foreign companies will have to entrust a local agent whenever not in possession of a Chinese business license and address.

The International application on the other hand, may be fully carried out in English, although more expensive, has some practical advantages. Among all the registrant has to render a sole request to the WIPO, this same request is then transmitted automatically to each and single trademark office for which the extension/s is required. Therefore, involving rather few interactions with national trademark offices—with sensible time reduction whenever the company intends to register world-wide or more technically in a great number of countries. This opportunity shall be evaluated whenever intended registration simultaneously involves several member States of the abovementioned convention (e.g. registration in Europe, some South American countries, Southeast Asia, China and India). Once the request is issued to WIPO and by it transmitted to all selected countries, then the same will finally become disjointed and separate, so it is very possible that result will be different in each country, some might accept, some might oppose it in both cases: fully or partially.

In the event of refusal of registration, in each country, the registrant has the right to request a review of the same decision. In this case, the additional costs to deal with these separate procedures, in term of both resources and time, should be taken into consideration while opting for this type of registration over the domestic one.

In consideration of the above, whereas China is the main point of interest in trademark registration, the purely domestic process shall be assessed instead. Although it may seem more difficult, opting for national registration has a substantial advantage, it allows to obtain—comparatively faster—the trademark registration certificate written in Chinese language, which could be also decisive in speeding up the interactions with local authorities or act in Court against infringements more promptly. In addition, the domestic procedure is less costly compared to the international one.

Finally, although the national and the international registration are both based on the Nice Classification, it shall be pointed out that peculiarly in addition to international principles—the protection of trademarks in China recognizes "subclasses" also known as "items" that have an independent relevance and they must be specified in filling the application. It is crucial to carefully consider also this aspect while submitting an application, to avoid possible unintended consequences. For instance, Nice class no. 9, which has a broad scope covering from "scientific research devices" to "video games" is divided in Chinese system into 24 different subcategories. Therefore, when registering a trademark, it is important to ensure that registration covers products and services of all subclasses that might be related to one company's core business and consider also future possible expansion of the same business locking down relevant categories (this is about to slightly change considering the new "non-use" doctrine, discussed below).

In the light of the above, it is advisable to carefully select sub-category or item of registration: otherwise the gap will be filled by the office itself and this is to be considered detrimental to the success of the registration itself. There is in fact a risk that the officer in charge, in case of a lack of clarification by the applicant, will independently select some subclasses not necessarily related to the applicant's activity, thus unnecessarily widening the possibilities of rejecting the application itself or to accidentally conflict with an existing registration—which may be avoided with a careful selection of the proper items. The same conduct furthermore exposes the company to the risk of obtaining partial coverage of the subclasses in which its really interested in selling product and/or providing services.

3.5 Language

In registering a trademark in China, language is one of the most complicated aspects. Registration of one non-figurative mark can be applied within the system either in Latin alphabet or Chinese characters (or both) but always separately. The opportunity to register the first or the latter (or both) shall be always cautiously evaluated.

Firstly, shall be noted that Chinese characters registration is not mandatory; in case shall be requested by a separate registration (for each Nice class—therefore extra or double costs are to be evaluated as well), but undeniably in specific cases it could grant an extra degree of protection.

However, in case a foreign commercial operator wishes to register its non-figurative trademark in Chinese characters shall seek the advice of a domestic marketing firm, entrust mother tongue consultant or highly skilled professional translator. Generally speaking, it is advisable to seek for professional advice in order to translate company/mark name into Chinese character or either identify a new set of characters (normally no more than 3–4 as an exception) which shall represent the company name within the Chinese market, possibly whenever read shall be phonetically similar to the English or foreign language pronunciation of the brand name to do not dilute the market appeal as already built—at the same time—in best practices, transmit an appealing message to the consumer through the subtle meaning of each selected characters.

These actions and considerations might seem superfluous, but on the contrary we shall consider that they constitute a way to control and design local understating of a company brand in this specific market. In addition, it shall be considered that this phenomenon will happen anyway whether the commercial operator want it or not. Local consumers, clients or competitors will anyway 'bestow' an equivalent name in Chinese for a company or a brand name if spelled in English—especially in the more rural area of the Country, where business is carried out exclusively in Chinese.

A very successful example of the above, is the transliteration given by a famous American beverage brand to its most famous product, soda cans. The four characters chosen to compose the name, other than producing a similarity with the English pronunciation, provide an added value in terms of meaning reflecting the characteristic of the product resulting in a perfect marketing operation, if considered singularly and read it together the four characters used to spell the name sound exactly like the brand name but roughly reads as "happiness in/for your mouth" or "drinking it will make you happy" (to be more precise: "permitting the mouth to rejoice").

On the other hand, among the famous western brands that entered the Chinese market in the past years, we can also identify several cases of potential risk related to a careless administration of the intellectual property matter. Among many, most exemplificative might be cases involving a famous French fashion company and a pharmaceutical group known for its product used also in erectile disfunction treatments.

In the first case involving the French fashion house, following the lack of registration of its Chinese denomination already spread among the consumers, the registration was finally made by a Chinese local enterprise. As a response, the fashion company tried to apply for the recognition of the trademark as "well-known trademark" also trying, in the meantime, to register a name with the same pronunciation but with a different Chinese character, as an alternative to the one already registers. In order to get an alternative registration and possibly obtain separately invalidation of the first mark registered by the local company in Court.

After applications for Well-known trademark at the time even more hard to be obtained (dispute dates back to 1997) and the 'alternative pronunciation' registration were both rejected, the French company could not allowed to use the Chinese denomination, as already used by its consumers. In the meantime, the name could have been rightfully used by the holder of registration in Mainland china for commercial purposes in the same territory. The legal dispute was taken to Court and lasted very long without bringing very satisfying results.

Similar issues related to Chinese characters registration may be found in the case involving the pharmaceutical group, even if the lack of trademark registration was less deliberate. Specifically, the product was commercialized through unofficial channels without any permission provided by the group, and therefore the same company was not aware of the matter. Basically, in this case, the denomination in Chinese characters already spread among the consumers, but as a consequence of third-party unauthorized trade in the region. The denomination—that phonetically has a very similar pronunciation of the original name—represents a very successful translation as, other than the phonetic similarity, included an appealing meaning that also recall the product qualities. The name (that can be approximately translated as "powerful elder brother") was very likely to be remembered by the consumer, adding a strong value in terms of marketing and image return.

In performing its official debut in the Chinese market, occurred after the name registration of its product as a trademark by a third party, the pharmaceutical group had no other choice but to register an alternative name. However, it was not very successful among the public, as the other name was already well known to general public. Company was not able to trade and exploit popularity of its most renown product name due to the conflicting registration that barred it to trade under the name as translated in Chinese and as known by its consumers.

Proceeding anyway with the production and trading of its own products would have brought disastrous consequences, since the trademark was already registered by third parties. Nowadays can be even more dangerous, as the intellectual property protection is even more enforced, compare to the last decade.

A famous French wine company was involved in this specific scenario and was compelled to compensate the local distributor paying a 4-million-euro compensation for trading under its company name translated in Chinese which was in fact a trademark already registered by the distributor. This almost absurd scenarios could have different outcomes in the future, if related to a bad faith registration (particularly last example), as the new Trademark law, in force from November 1, 2019 provide renovated protection. Malicious act carried out by the applicant or by the agent that facilitate the registration, are more sanctioned. Improvements have been done also regarding the recognition of the "well-known trademark" compare to the prior decade.

When facing one of the circumstances described above, it is always advisable to contact a specialized professional to assist the company on the related matter. Moreover, help could be provided by marketing and communication experts to build the correct image of its own brand and products. Choosing the right Chinese denomination it is particularly important, not only for the pronunciation and the meaning behind it but also for the choice of the Chinese characters that can have a huge impact on the brand reputation and even on the entire trading operation.

3.6 Registration Procedure, Opposition, Invalidation and Cancellation for Non-use

Here follows a brief analysis on registration procedure and related protection tools.

Registration—The CNIPA processes and examine request in a chronological order considering the specific filling time.

Usually, each application is examined within 90 days from the filing. In any case, the relevant office shall provide an official reply within nine months. Once the application is examined, if there are not previous conflicting registrations, the office proceeds by publishing the application on the official register, allowing third parties to check and eventually to submit opposition. If no opposition is rendered within the time frame of three months from publication, the registration procedure is finalized, and the certificate issued. Protection is from this moment onwards fully in effect.

Opposition—previously, the opposition could be lodged by anyone. This allowed the gradual increase of futile or bad-faith oppositions. Under the current regime normally only vested subject and priority or pre-emptive right holders (anyway enjoying a particular connection with the disputed right) are admitted proposing an opposition to the registration. Only under the following special circumstances other subjects (as third parties) may also file an opposition, when the registration to be opposed concerns a trademark which is: (a) similar to a not-yet registered but recognized "well-known trademark" for identical or similar products; (b) similar to a registered "well-known trademark" for different products; (c) filed by not authorized agents; (d) it has a misleading geographic indication. Similarly, the right to oppose lays generally on all subjects, whenever a registration is against specific law provisions (e.g. everyone can oppose a "black swastika with ethic offenses logo" to be registered in a certain class).

Considering that last amendments of Trademark law introduced the general prohibition to maliciously register a trademark with intent of "no-use", this case now also falls in the latter category of general right to oppose registration. In this regard we shall note that, the law does not specify the benchmarks for the bad faith registration which is defined by judicial interpretations. The principles have been defined by the High Court of Beijing that highlighted some typical bad faith registration scenarios (for example: the simultaneous application of different trademarks in different classes, that show a lack of connection between them and the subject who apply for the registration).

Regarding the effects of the procedure against the opposed mark, until the formal invalidation of the trademark, the same can be rightfully used. The entire procedure by law shall be concluded within 12 months.

Whenever the competent office decides in favour of the opposing party, the defendant can either firstly apply for review within the Trademark Office and if not satisfied, eventually bring the matter to Court (having applied for review is not mandatory, and court remedies can be accessed even directly after opposition decision).

On the other hand, if the decision is not in favour of the opposing party, the same party is not admitted to request review, but can always bring the matter to the attention of the competent Court. Finally, in case of rejection of the opposition no matter if the judicial procedure is activated, the competent office will directly issue the registration certificate of the trademark while in the past, the issuance was postponed until conclusion of the eventual judicial procedure as activated.

All review procedure against opposition, declaration of invalidity, revocation, cancellation, for prior existing marks or in conflict against a well-known trademark shall be concluded within nine to twelve months, time frames which are mandatory but they can be extended by decision of the trademark office from three to six months depending on actual circumstances.

Moreover, if the CNIPA rejects the application for trademark registration, the applicant shall present an opposition to that decision to the TRAB within fifteen days after the receipt of the related notification. In case of positive outcome for the applicant, the CNIPA shall purse with application and issue the related certificate in due time. In case the same opposition is rejected, the applicant may seek remedies in Court of law within thirty days beginning from the related notification receipt.

Invalidation—in case the opposition time frame has expired, a mark may be invalidated by filing a request to the CNIPA and competent office, whenever such trademark (either):

(i) is a reproduction, imitation or transliteration of a "well-known trademark";
(ii) has been registered by an agent without proper authorization;
(iii) contains an indication of origin that is untrue and deviant for the consumers;
(iv) infringes the rights of the previous owner of the trademark.

The application shall be filed within five years from the mark registration date, the time limitation does not apply whereas the trademark to be invalidated conflict with a well-known trademark.

As presented in the previous paragraphs, the 2014 reform introduced for the first time in China an important principle that is now one of the fundamental principles regulating the matter: all trademarks must be registered according to the principles of good faith, honesty and integrity. In addition, if a registration request is similar to a trademark (even if not registered in China) which the applicant had entertained business relations with, the same request shall be rejected.

In this way, it will be possible to oppose and obtain rejection as an exception of the first to file principle, if a bad faith registration occurred. It is crucial however to be able to prove the existence of a trade relationship. The same decision can be appealed in Court within 30 days from the reception of the related notice.

The new Trademark Law (2019) also add the bad faith registration with intent of non-use among the reason of invalidation (within five years from the registration) while before this remedy could not be accessed in such cases and trademark squatting issues were to be addressed only after a certain amount of period passed without use of the same mark beginning from registration (specifications just below, regarding bad faith registration criteria please refer to the quoted High Court Guidelines just above).

Cancellation for non-use—another tool of protection against a Company trademark in conflict with other trademarks as previously registered is the cancellation for non-use since in China the use of a registered trademark is mandatory, the request may be filed three years after registration, if the registrant fail to prove such use, the mark shall be consequently invalidated. To prove the non-use, an investigation report or situation status has to be filed together with the application. After that, the burden of proof will be shifted to the trademark owner who needs to prove the real business use of the trademark during the past three years, starting from registration or either if more time has passed counting back from request for non-use cancellation. In practice evidence of use shall contain at least the following elements:

(i) date and place of use;
(ii) trademark;
(iii) username;
(iv) particular class of good and services as contested.

In particular fail to prove point (iv) as above, may lead to partial invalidation that might reveal as much satisfactory as a full invalidation, in fact, many times the conflicting mark is blocking one registration just as a consequence of unintentional abuse of registration (trademark was registered in many different classes or subclasses) where the real business of one company do not normally happens in that extend. All the above evidence use might be contested; however, they are easily fabricated.

In fact, by "use" to be proven, is commonly intended as "use over a product, packaging and containers, or on business documents, advertising campaigns, during exhibitions or other business-related activities". This definition—introduced by the Trademark Law reform—was contested as it could represent am additional advantage for the trademark squatters. By defining the term "use", defending a squatter is less difficult as they can avoid the trademark cancellation just by using it in a simple advertise to interrupt the 3 years period necessary to demonstrate the non-use. As previously reported, the non-cancellation was, since last trademark law reform, one of the few solutions against the abusive practices of bad faith registration. Entities that register multiple trademarks, most of the time do not intend to commercialize the products but want to obtain a financial benefit by selling the trademark to the legitimate owner.

In case the registration is not malicious, but the effective non-use persists (such as the case explained above of over-registration of many superfluous categories) it remains the best (if not the only) remedy to enter the market or solve potential conflicts.

Procedure of non-use cancellation is mainly divisible in three separate steps (according to outcomes and parties will). Firstly, procedure shall be filled within the CNIPA and the authority will notify the targeted company which shall be called to prove actual use of the contested trademark submitting related evidences. After examination CNIPA will render a decision. Either party dissatisfied with the decision can apply for review with TRAB, here more opportunity to challenge evidence of use is given. TRAB will render a decision based on the cross-examination of evidence as submitted by the parties. The result of this decision can be reviewed in Court, in this case the unsatisfied party may file a claim to the Beijing IP Court. Either of the parties shall be a plaintiff, the other party shall be the third party in the dispute, consequently the TRAB shall be always the resistant to the claim. If any of the three parties, are dissatisfied with the first instance ruling, they may apply for appeal to the High Court in Beijing as final instance.

There are indeed some negative aspects: firstly, the three years before which the remedy may not be accessed. Secondly, to be successful the requesting party shall be certain up some degree that the targeted party is not actually using the trademark, otherwise the application can be very easily rejected.

In addition, prior the request, it is always recommended to conduct investigations activities to understand the real identity of the applicant and its intentions to better adopt tailored solutions. An investigation might highlight for instance that: (a) a company is active but do not trade in that particular segment in conflict with the mark we intend to register; (b) the registrant is an individual-serial squatter that registered many trademarks in many different classes and most likely will not have done any commercialization or official promotion (for cost reasons). If the entity is a company and it is active, make sure to check if it is under "abnormal activities" (liquidation) for more than three years. With the previous three outcome of investigation, non-use cancellation shall be always attempted.

3.7 Malicious Practices, Good Faith Principle

The recent reforms respond to the demand of protection and to the limitation of abusive practices. These practices have been spreading faster and faster since the 2000s, with public disclosure of information contained in the CNIPA registry. The research system of registered trademarks, as a matter of fact, has been also utilized to identify the possible target of malicious registration. Such registrations are usually operated by individuals or sole-shareholders shelter companies, whose main purpose is obtaining trademark registration to exploit the consequent transfer of rights to the 'legitimate' owner.

This possibility represents a clear obstacle for foreign companies. The owners of a given trademark registered in China by third parties faces manly two choices:

- regaining their trademark through judicial action and/or negotiation;
- find a new registrable sign among the possible alternatives (e.g. Latin and/or Chinese characters) which may be similar—with evident limitations of similarity with the registered mark, or totally different.

The latter option may be advisable for small enterprises with no goodwill or no past presence in China. However, this might implicate significant costs (e.g. costs for the trademark design and packaging; besides possible additional manufacturing on single products; the non-usability of the previously stored goods that bear the squatted trademark; delays in production, etc.).

The same procedure cannot be applied to companies that are already renowned in the East, as they would be compelled to rebuild their position in the Chinese market from scratch.

Regarding bad faith, it shall be noted that the new law provides for trademark registration and its usage, establishing the clear duty for the party to abide correctness and good faith.

The new law introduced the bad faith registration as independent circumstance that if present is sufficient for CNIPA to reject registration. This new provision shall decrease future squatting also considering that the same can be claimed also in invalidation, while prior modification a squatted trademark could only be cancelled by non-use.

After the new amendments implementation there are numerous solutions against the abusive practice of trademark squatting if compared to the prior system. Firstly, this form of protection exerts its effects automatically when setting forth that “the registration in bad faith with the intention of non-use must be rejected”. Secondary, in case the registration in bad faith is not rejected, it is possible to deploy in sequence opposition and invalidation, having always the chance to request the cancellation due to non-use (this had been the only possible solution for such specific cases until 2019).

These new principles of protection result as new duties for third parties which are involved in the procedure, i.e. trademark agents and CNPIA. Since 2019, in fact, the administrative authorities must guarantee both confidentiality of the information received from registrant, and they have in addition the duty to reject such registration when requested in bad faith.

The same obligation, in term of respect of confidentiality and not allowing third parties to register in bad faith with the intent of non-use are imposed also onto trademark agents that from now on shall play a more vigilant role regarding applications as proposed via their office and practice. In order to enforce these duties, the law imposes administrative measures and sanctions, as well as more grave fines, against agencies that willingly support such malicious registration.

The above-mentioned regulations might soon be strengthened. During the redaction of this text, the CNIPA has published a draft on Implementation rules to be applied the procedure of trademarks registration. The text indicates possible future scenarios of the evolution of trademark registration procedure, with particular regard to the abusive practice issue. It highlights some criteria in order to identify bad-faith registration actions and attitude, prescribing when the same acts constitutes an index of bad faith; it also provides a sort of squatter blacklist to forbid future registration from the same subjects, as well as the application on sanction inspired by the social credit system (e.g. double-speed registration evaluation process). For the above, it is predicable that the current squatting situation might be reduced in the years to come.

3.8 Well-Known Trademark

Under specific circumstances, during civil proceedings involving trademark protection against counterfeiting, or during administrative proceedings it is possible to request the status of "well-known trademark". If this status is recognized, the trademark will benefit of a wider protection extended also to classes and services not related to the registered ones.

It is important to notice that an official "well-known trademark" record does not exist. This status is recognized individually by the administrative or judicial authorities, requiring a specific recognition by the same.

The criteria provided by law for the recognition of the well-known status are several and not cumulative. Authorities shall evaluate the degree of awareness of the trademark among the target audience, the good reputation it has, the period of its "use", the geographic area in which it is promoted and if the status has been already recognized in other countries.

The new Trademark law extends protection to such trademarks, with no regards if they are registered in China or not. Therefore, the Chinese legislation stipulate that it is not allowed to register or use in any way, for the same type of goods, a similar trademark where it can result misleading consumers or either may cause harm to the owner of the well-known trademark.

On the other hand, if the trademark was registered also in China, the protection is even wider. For Chinese registered well known trademarks for instance, the time limitation of five years for Invalidation of conflicting trademarks, do not apply. Even if this status is hard to obtain (the criteria are very narrow and the possibilities to obtain it from a foreign company is even harder) there are sensible improvements also in this field.

In fact, since the first recognition of this status to a foreign company (a famous American F&B brand), the criteria and the process itself evolved. According to most recent judicial interpretation and case studies, main points may be recognized as follow: it is crucial to prove that the trademark is geographically renown over the PRC territory (for example in 15 provinces); the use and knowledge of the trademark for a period of time lasted at least for a sensible period of time (for example 2 years). To increase the possibilities for the recognition of the status, it is required a well-organized and planned operation with the help of an expert to successfully collect all the elements, sales records, invoices of commercials aired or displayed within the territory, contracts of license within the territory (if any).

The most difficult part for an applicant in well-known trademark recognition is to submit enough evidence proving that his trademark has become well-known. The evidence should prove the reputation of the applicant's mark before the date of filing of the disputed mark or before the date of the alleged use. The evidence has almost necessarily to be formed in mainland of China (excluding Hong Kong and Macao), because the reputation in other jurisdiction is deemed as a mere reference.

Finally we remind that by law, the well-known trademark right holders should be aware that they cannot directly use the words "well-known trademark" on their goods and the packages or containers of their goods or for advertisements, exhibitions, and other commercial activities, since the law forbids such uses in order not ingenerate confusion.

In addition, it shall be noted that recently the "well-known trademark" status has been also extended to web domains by specific regulations.

Chapter 4
Copyright

4.1 Definition

In each legal system Copyright is intended as the right(s) of the author on its literary and artistic creations as recognized and sanctioned by law. A right granted by statute to the author or originator of certain literary and/or artistic productions, of which he/she is invested, for a specific time frame, with the sole and exclusive privilege of reproduce copies of the same, modifying, publishing and selling them.

The right might be registered yet it originates by act of creation (i.e. as defined by the Berna Convention "as soon as the work is fixed"), time frame of granted protection, condition to retain or extend the right vary in different legal system.

Contrary to the plain definition and the most common understood implementation of the right, i.e. the pure exploitation of artists' creations, registered copyright could be intended also as useful tool to protect intellectual property of a given company.

In fact, enterprises create everyday original material and distinctive creations that might have an extensive market value like product models, preparatory sketches, software, or simply other written documents, promotional material, catalogues, newsletters, website content, photos, brochure (even if not related to its main business) of which the company might wish to be the sole authorized user or better exclude third parties and competitors from reproducing and exploiting it.

The core principle of Copyright law essentially is to protect right of the authors of certain "Works" and "Creative Works" shall those be related to their reputation or their commercial exploitation.

The Copyright Law of PRC do not define the exact scope of "Work" as protected under the law. A more detailed definition may be found within the provisions of the "Implementation Regulation of the Copyright Law of the People Republic of China" (2013) "Implementation Rules 2013". Articles 2 and 3 of the Implementation rules specify that "Works" as stated in the Copyright law shall include "*original works of literature, arts and sciences, with intellectual results which can be reproduced in a tangible form*". Article 3, the term "creative works" as stated in the Copyright Law

G. Pisacane and D. Zibetti, *Intellectual Property in China*, China Law, Tax & Accounting,
https://doi.org/10.1007/978-981-15-4558-0_4

shall include "*intellectual activities directly related to the production of works, literature and science*". For a complete set of definitions, including but not limited to the identification of "literary works" "musical works" "artistic works" "cinematography works" "audio recordings".

4.2 Law and Regulations

The modern legal framework it was implemented in China thirty years ago.

The Copyright Law of the People's Republic of China was firstly promulgated on September 7th, 1990. It was then amended twice, specifically, in 2001 and again in 2010. The Law is currently undergoing a process of further reform, new amendment draft was published in 2018 and is awaiting for the final deliberation of the National People's Congress which is expected for the end of the 13th session of its Standing Committee (potentially before the end of 2020, deliberation date to be confirmed).

Beside the Copyright law, the related implementing regulations were issued in 2013. As in many other fields these rules constitute a fundamental part of the legislation on copyright protection in China. Beside the Implementation rules 2013 which generally address the matter, different sets of specific rules concerning copyright issues have issued separately by the State Council. Among those, the Regulations for the Protection of Computer Software (third and last amendment in 2013) set forth basics for copyright protection of software. The mentioned software regulations provide for renting and lease of software and define also administrative sanctions for unauthorized distribution and sales of software online. Furthermore, the "NAC" (National Administration of Copyright) issued the Measures for the Administrative Protection of Internet Copyright in 2005 setting out administrative duties of service providers which distribute content through the internet.

The SPC has also issued various judicial interpretations which now constitute a fundamental part of copyright protection.

For civil litigation, the SPC issued the Interpretations concerning the application of Laws in the Trial of Civil Disputes over Copyrights. As well as a separate opinion on the "Infringement of the Right of Communication through Information Networks" (effective from January 1st, 2013).

The same SPC in 2004, jointly with the SPC Procuratorate (PRC highest Procurator, which during the years released many valuable interpretations) issued a judicial opinion that set out limits for the criminalization of potential acts of infringement explicitly drawing differences in the thresholds of online and offline acts of Infringement. Furthermore, online acts were formally recognized as potential criminal offence by this very act. The related threshold was then lowered by a further opinion issued in few years later in 2007. The same two judicial bodies issued also another very useful joint interpretation providing for criminal investigation jurisdiction over cases involving internet piracy.

Finally, as the world's majority of States China is member of the Berne Convention for the Protection of Literary and Artistic Works (1886) consequentially its provisions are fully in force within the territory of PRC. Worth noting that this very same convention set forth the widely recognized principle cited in the paragraph above regarding the moment of existence of the copyright.

The administrative framework is composed of national and local level of entities that supervise application of the law and regulations, as well as the actual enjoyment of the copyrights and their related issues, the same copyright law design such scheme of national and local level of protection. National level highest authority is the abovementioned National Administration of Copyright. NCA is affiliated to State Administration of Press, Publication, Radio, Film and Television. At local level, within each local bureau competent for Culture, Broadcasting and Television communications, there is a special division which manage copyright enforcement. Those divisions operate under different names which vary locally, yet with similar (and quite limited) functions.

4.3 Scope of Protection

The Copyright law identifies entities and works covered by its provisions.

In these respects, for the firsts Article 2 specifies that "*works of Chinese citizens, legal persons or other organizations shall, regardless if they are published or not, enjoy copyright pursuant to this Law*" therefore, recognizing the application and the right of exploitation to any of the enlisted legal entities other than individuals, physical person authors. The same Article 2 further provides regarding Foreigners and Stateless person, extending to them the same rights upon certain conditions. In fact, copyrights of Foreigners and Stateless person are (for instance) recognized and protected in China whereas the home country is part of an international treaty of which China is also signatory (e.g. Berna Convention) or otherwise whereas a bilateral treaty between China and the author's home country have entered a bilateral treaty and more extensions related to treaties and convention which applies simultaneously in China and in the State of the 'habitual residence of the author'. Significantly, the law also extends protection to works of Foreigners (and Stateless person) if firstly published in China, or according to the implementation rules, even if not 'firstly' published in China but however published within 30 days. For the complete list of copyright extensions, the last part of Article 2 provides.

As per the works that entitles the author to enjoy the related copyrights Article 3 provides that works referred to Copyright law "*shall include literature, art and natural science, social science, engineering and technical works created in the following forms:*"

(i) Written works;
(ii) Oral works;
(iii) Musical, dramatic, opera, dance, acrobatic artistic work;
(iv) Art, architectural works;
(v) Photographic works;

(vi) Film works and works created using methods similar to film making;
(vii) Graphic works and model works such as engineering design plan, product design plan, map, schematic diagrams;
(viii) Computer software; and
(ix) Any other works stipulated by laws and administrative regulations.

Finally, Article 5 provide that the same law shall not apply to "*laws, regulations, decisions of State agencies*" administrative and judicial bodies, official translation thereof; current affair news; general tables; general forms and formulas.

It shall be noted that, firstly scope of protection is quite extensive. It potentially covers many fields of art, science and technical applications. As reported above, these aspect also involves daily operations of many if not all business entities and in this perspective, register a copyright (possibly jointly with Patent, design patent or other IP registration—registrability may vary from case to case) in China may increase dramatically protection of the same valuable intellectual property.

In summary we might note that, PRC citizens including legal persons and other organizations enjoy the most extended protection of their copyright in China, wheatear published or not. Foreigners (and Stateless persons on the other hand, enjoys copyright protection under PRC law for works published in China, and subsidiary or supplementary protection of the same copyright law for works published outside China pursuant to (a) an international convention which both their home country and China ratified; or (b) a bilateral agreement concluded between China and their home country/country of habitual residence. Under these conditions, the overall protection is almost equally recognized and largely accessible.

As per the scope of author's right, China recognizes a quite wide set of the same pertaining to the person and reputation of the author or related to the nature or exploitation (also commercial) of the work.

In fact, by law Copyright (Article 10) shall include the following personal rights and property rights, here resumed:

(i) Publication rights, i.e. the rights to decide whether a work is made public or not;
(ii) Right of Authorship, or the right to be named as the author of the work.
(iii) Right of Revision, i.e. the right to revise a work or to authorise other to revise the same;
(iv) Right to preserve the integrity of a work, i.e. the right to protect a work from distortion or tampering (complementary to no. 3);
(v) Reproduction right, i.e. the right to reproduce one or more copies of a work by printing, photocopying, audio and/or video recording, duplication, photographic reproduction (law includes an open "etc.");
(vi) Distribution right, i.e. the right to provide the original copy or replicas of a work to the public by sale or as gift;
(vii) Rental right, i.e. the right to license the temporary use of film works, works created using methods similar to film making and computer software by other for a fee, except where the computer software is the main subject of the fee.

(viii) Exhibition right, i.e. the right to put the original copy or replicas of art works and photographic works on public display;
(ix) Performance right, i.e. the right to put up a public performance of a work and publicly broadcast performance of work through various means;
(x) Screening right, i.e. the right to put up a public screening of art works, photographic works, film works, works created using methods similar to film making, etc. through technical equipment such as film projector, slide projector, and so on;
(xi) Broadcasting right, i.e. the right to publicly broadcast or transmit a work through wireless method, the right to transmit or broadcast a work to the public through cable or relay broadcast, and the right to transmit or broadcast a work to the public through a loudspeaker or other tools for transmission of symbols, sounds and images;
(xii) Information network transmission right, i.e. the right to provide a work to the public through cable or wireless method so that the public may have access to the work at their individually selected time and venue;
(xiii) Filming right, i.e. the right to produce a work on a medium through film making or methods similar to film making;
(xiv) Adaptation right, i.e. the right to adapt a work, thus creating a new work with originality;
(xv) Translation right, i.e. the right to convert the written text of a work from one language to another language;
(xvi) Compilation right, i.e. the right to select or arrange a work or parts of a work for compilation into a new work;
(xvii) Any other right enjoyed by copyright holder.

In considering numbers here enlisted from (i) to (xvii) we shall note that the same could be divided in two macroscopic categories. Also in consideration of the other provisions of the law pertaining them, rights as indicated by numbers from (i) to (iv) could be defined as a minimum core of rights, of which the author is permanently vested of or, entitle to, that refers specifically to creative and artistic aspects of the work; while number from (v) onwards relates more to commercial aspects of the copyright.

Pertaining fees, the same article also provides for licensing affirming the right of the author to receive the related fee. In this regard law specifies that a Copyright holder may license to other the exercise of the reproduction rights (item no. v) and any other right enjoyed by the same (item no. xvii) and receive remuneration pursuant to the related agreement. If no agreement was made or signed, the law provide an alternative and secondary mechanism to protect copyright holder which is by the same law entitled to receive such fees whenever licensing the above rights.

The same holder may also transfer the above-identified rights (no. v and/or xvii) as specified by the last paragraph of Article 10. It shall be noted that the difference between the two alienation of rights resides in the time frame of such assignments. While licensing is temporary, transfer is permanent.

Transfer of ownership of a work and related rights are to be consider separately. In this respect the law specifically provides for transfer of ownership of "original piece of art". Article 18 provides that the act of transfer or anyhow sell one original piece of art to a buyer do not transfer automatically any copyright from the author to the buyer, except for the right to display (or rent to display) such original piece of art.

4.4 Attribution

PRC Copyright law provides a general principle of attribution of copyright to the author of the work, specifically (Article 11) "*Copyright shall belong to the author, unless otherwise stipulated by this law. The author of a work shall be the citizen who has created the work*".

Where no evidence is provided, author shall be deemed the individual (or the entity) whom name is stated on the work. This principle establishes the obligation for any claimant to actively prove its allegation over ownership of a work a circumstance, which is very common in practice, whether the copyright is used without registration, or during and/or against registration procedure.

In case the work is jointly created the same law recognizes the principle of "co-authoring". For multiple authors, it is provided by the implementing regulations that co-authors shall find an agreement to define limits of exploitation or enjoyment of their separate right of use as they are entitled of. In case of lack of such agreement, they shall freely enjoy those rights separately without influencing the full enjoyment of the others. In this respect shall be noted that, a serious act of influence over co-author enjoyment or restriction thereof, such granting as exclusive license agreement to a third party, shall be enacted upon permission of all co-authors. Additionally, it shall be noted that separate users shall account for any gain of the copyright, fairly report it to them and share all related profits with co-authors. In practice might be advisable to conclude a detailed agreement with all co-authors as soon as possible, before registration and/or exploitation of the related rights.

As reported below authors may not be only physical persons. A legal entity such as a company might very well be considered author under Chinese law. In fact, the same copyright law provide that where the creation of a work is sponsored by, decided by, and is responsibility of a legal person, entity or other kind of organization, the same shall be deemed as "author" and enjoy the related copyright.

The work shall be therefore deemed as legal entity's work.

In other cases, as delimited by the same law copyrights are divided by either law provisions or agreement between the involved parties. In particular we refer to work "in course of employment" and "commissioned work".

The difference lays in the nature of the relationship between the subject who sponsor or request the execution of a work and the executor. In the first instance, a work made "in course of employment" is defined by the law as a work created by an individual in order to accomplish a task assigned to him by an employer. As general principle copyright related to such works belongs to the employee with some exception set out by the Copyright law.

As for instance, under any of the following circumstances the employer shall be vested of the copyright while the author shall retain mere authorship, specifically if work is related to:

(i) drawing of engineering designs, drawing of product designs, maps, software, etc., created mainly by using the technical material and the resources of a legal person or other entity and the responsibility for which is borne by the legal person or other organization.
(ii) Whereas the copyright for the "work for hire" is assigned to the employer by law, administrative regulations or by a contract between the employer and the employee.

It should be noted that basic criteria for such separation between execution and enjoyment of copyrights revolves mainly on (a) use of resources/material of a different entity; (b) agreement between the party or special law provisions (which will be examined below—e.g. as provided for film making and movies).

As for commissioned works, similar to "work in course of employment" (point 2, just above) the commission contract shall regulate the attribution of the work produced under commission. In case of lack of specific provisions regarding it, the copyright shall be enjoyed by the commissioned party. Considering the above provisions, it is strongly advisable to establish and carefully negotiate the aspects thereof in advance.

As previously reported, other special provision for attribution are explicitly provided by the law. For instance, Article 12 provides "*the copyright of a work created from adaptation, translation, annotation or collation of an existing work shall belong to the person who undertakes adaptation, translation, annotation or collation*" provided that the copyright of the original work shall not be infringed at the time of exercise of copyright by the person who undertakes the adaptation, translation, annotation or collation. As noted above, infringement shall be demonstrated by the claimant also proving its own vested rights. Article 14 provide for shared authorship and division of shared works and related rights. Among complex works including different IP rights from several authors cooperating in one project, the law specifically provides for movies (film works and similar works created using methods similar to film making) related rights shall belong to the producers; however—specify the law—the playwright, director, photographer, lyricist, composer, who have the right of authorship shall have the right to receive remuneration pursuant to the contract executed with the producer. For scripts, soundtrack, score and other similar works that might be independently used in film works and created with similar methods, related authors they shall have the right to exercise his/her copyright separately.

4.5 Permission, Limitations and Exceptions

By law use of work (commercial or not) shall require permission of the vested entity, or licensing thereof and as reported, the related fees shall be paid accordingly.

However, the legal framework identifies certain circumstances under which the mere use of a work not requires licensing by the rightful owner and the related remuneration need not to be paid, provided that the name of the author and the title of the work shall be stated, and other rights enjoyed by the copyright holder pursuant to Copyright law shall not be infringed:

(i) Use of a work published by others for personal learning, research or appreciation.
(ii) Appropriate citation of a work published by others in a work for the purpose of introduction or commentary of a certain work or explanation of a certain issue;
(iii) Inevitable reproduction or citation of a published work on media such as newspapers, periodicals, radio stations, television stations, etc. for reporting of current affairs news;
(iv) Publication or broadcast by media such as newspapers, periodicals, radio stations, television stations, etc. of articles on current affairs pertaining to politics, economics, religious issues published by other media such as newspapers, periodicals, radio stations, television stations, etc., except where the author has stated that publication or broadcast is not permitted;
(v) Publication or broadcast by media such as newspapers, periodicals, radio stations, television stations, etc. of speeches made at public meetings, except where the author has stated that publication or broadcast is not permitted;
(vi) Translation or replication in small quantity of published works for use by teaching or scientific research personnel in classroom teaching or scientific research at schools, provided that publication and distribution shall be prohibited;
(vii) Use of published works by State agencies within a reasonable scope for execution of official duties;
(viii) Replication by libraries, archives, memorials, museums, art galleries, etc. of works collected by them for the purpose of display or preservation;
(ix) Gratis performance of published works to the public for free and no remuneration is paid to the performers;
(x) Copying, drawing, photographing and video recording of art works installed or displayed at outdoor public premises.
(xi) Translation of Chinese language works published by Chinese citizens, legal persons or any other organisations into minority language works for publication and distribution in China; and Translation of published works into Braille for publication.

As explicitly set forth by the same article—the provisions of the above paragraph apply also to restriction of rights of publishers, performers, producers of audio-visual recordings, radio stations and television stations. Regarding the above entities, law provides some limitation on their specific use author's copyright. The use of others' works by publishers, performers, producers of audio-visual recordings, radio stations, television stations (etc.,) pursuant to the relevant provisions of Copyright law shall not infringe the author's right of:

- Authorship
- right of revision,
- right to preserve the integrity of work; and
- right to receive remuneration.

This shall be understood as the minimum core of rights of which every author is entitled to preserve by law, if not agreed or permitted by him/her otherwise.

As per time limitation of copyright protection it should be noted that period of protection of right of authorship, right of revision, right to preserve the integrity of work (as also enlisted in Article 10, no. 1 to no. 3—Copyright law examined above) shall not be subjected to any time limitations. Quite similar provisions might be found in the vast majority of legal systems, clearly enough their scope is to protect the creative aspects of a work and reputation of the author that permanently retains the right to present to third parties the exact same work as by him/her intended not allowing unintended modification of author's work perpetrated by third parties against its will.

Therefore, we shall note that the legal framework recognises unlimited time authorship rights (right not pertaining to commercial exploitation of the copyright).

On the contrary, for publication rights and the other commercial-related rights (as stressed before no. v to no. xvii of Article 10, Copyright law) Article 21 specifically provides that period of protection of the same rights shall be "*the entire life span of the author and 50 years following his/her death, and shall expire on 31 December of the 50*th *year following the author's death*" or in case of co-authors, following the death of the last surviving author. Legal entities are subjected to a similar provision that covers 50 years from the first date of publication of a work and expires December 31st of the 50th year after the first publication (if no work was published within the first 50 years after completion, it shall not enjoy any protection at all). The same rules applies also to rights connected to film works or works created with similar methods (disregarding if the actual author is an individual or a legal entity) and the related protection is granted until the 31st of December of the 50th year after first publication, with the same limitation reported for the legal entities: if no publication of the film work is made within the first 50 years, the work will not enjoy any protection at all.

During the above period of protection for individuals, in the events of death of the citizen that enjoys copyright law, the related rights enlisted in items (x) to (xvii) by Article 10 as entirely quoted above, ownership shall be transferred pursuant to provision of PRC, according to the Inheritance law and enjoyed for the remaining part and/or during the period of protection as established by the law (e.g. December 31st of the 50th year after author's death).

4.6 Registration of Copyright

As discussed above, under the current regime an author is vested with copyrights by the sole act of creating the work. The principle is supported by the ratification of China of the Berne Convention for the Protection of Literary and Artistic Works. Under these circumstances the registration of copyright is not, in any case, a precondition required for the enjoyment of the related rights, contrary to other Intellectual property rights related registrations in PRC, such as Trademark or Patent, which are absolutely required in order to claim infringement of the same rights and invoke protection thereof and/or obtain any related measures by the Court. For this reason, the Copyright registration process is named "Voluntary registration".

Although not mandatory, registration is still highly recommended. Such registration process, in fact, might be quite useful in case of dispute arising over the copyrights and furthermore to protect the author against claim of third parties that might challenge paternity i.e. authorship of a work, or again, to more easily activate an enforcement procedure in case of any enforcement and/or against any threat posed to the enjoyment of such rights.

As reported above, the registration certificate will be considered *prima facie* evidence of ownership in Court. Furthermore, the same certificate will grant several additional benefits here summarized again:

- Publicity of work, prima facie evidence of ownership (evidence remains disputable);
- Set a date of 'first publication' limiting dispute over protection's time limits;
- Increase possibilities of higher liquidation of damage (if added to other factors, in practice);
- Add value to the work in case of licensing or transfer;

Literary, Audio and Visual works are separately regulated for Computer software registrations.

Local (provincial) level of Copyright bureaus handle matter of registration within their own territorial jurisdiction, for Mainland citizen authors and domestic works. Bureaus operate under one national authority named National Copyright Administration of China (NCAC). Registrations involving foreign parties and parties from Hong Kong, Macau and Taiwan on the other hand, are handled separately by a different national entity, the Copyright Protection Centre of China (CPCC). Procedure are quite similar, fees are identical.

In both cases, applicant may be authors directly, or any other individual/entity holding a copyright, as well as owners of exclusive rights within the PRC or Copyrights holder's authorized agents.

Contrary to Trademark and Patent, the entrustment of an authorized local agent is not required to submit the application, however foreign operators shall take into consideration that although the application might be as well filled online (partially) and final part of the application might be very well finalized remotely mailing documents to the provide address, all steps of procedure are still exclusively in Chinese language. Therefore, guidance from an expert or assistance from mother tongue is still implicitly required.

Content of application may vary locally (different policies and requirements also in term of legalizations, number of copies, content and number of documents) and considering the relation between the applicant and the copyright to be registered. Author will have to provide mainly the works to be registered in the shape of photos, duplicate, copy of the original manuscripts, models other documents representing the works. In addition, holder of rights different from authors, will have to submit also the source i.e. license contract, copyright transfer agreement, furthermore, an agent will have to submit proof of authorization, such as a valid Power of Attorney. All categories above will have also to provide a valid identification document. The procedure starts with form submission and proof of payment of the registration fees, the latter three conditions are required for all type of registrants as indicated above.

Upon approval, the National Copyright Administration/or the China Copyright Protection Centre will issue copyright registration certificate. Ordinary procedure shall take 30 days from submission date, the competent office however, may delay and request integration of documents as submitted, in this case its response may be delayed for a total of two months.

In case of software registrations, special provisions regulate documents to be submitted. Among them, 30 pages of code are required to be submitted jointly with the application form. Considering the value embedded in these information that are required to be submitted, special rules are enacted in order to secure confidentiality and upon applicant request set forth conditions for submission in a special confidential registry for the software's source code and object code to be registered, under special circumstances and upon request this special submission might be sealed after examination.

4.7 Licensing, Transfer

Differences between license and transfer were analysed above in the previous chapters.

In regards of related agreements and method of transferring or licensing, the law specifies some special provisions in regards of minimum requirements for the content of such agreements, in some cases provides also a mandatory form of the same agreement (most commonly licensed items).

According to Article 24, a licence agreement shall include the following main contents:

(i) Definition of scope of rights licensed for usage;
(ii) Specification of the nature of rights licensed for usage in term of exclusivity of the same (exclusive or non-exclusive);
(iii) Geographical scope and time period of licensing usage;
(iv) Standards and method for payment of remuneration;

(v) Default liability; and
(vi) Any other contents deemed necessary by both parties to be agreed.

The same article for some specific licenses provides for mandatory written form, distinction is made according to their scope. For commercial rights (namely no. 5–17 as defined by Article 10 first paragraph), the related agreement shall be mandatorily concluded in written or deemed void.

According to Article 25, a transfer agreement shall contain at minimum:

(i) Name of the work;
(ii) Type of rights transferred, geographical scope;
(iii) Transfer price;
(iv) Date and method for payment of transfer price;
(v) Default liability; and
(vi) Any other contents deemed necessary by both parties to be agreed.

Notwithstanding if it is licensing or transferring a common rule for both is that the actual scope shall be considered as stated in the agreements between the parties. According to the same principle, any right not specified by the Copyright holder, might not be exercised by its counterparty in the license/transfer agreement without previous consent of the holder.

In general, when it comes to the right of use the law also provide that the counterparty shall not "not infringe the author's right of authorship, right of revision, right to preserve the integrity of work and right to receive remuneration." Those provisions specifically address those rights that are inherited with the creation of works and of which the creator i.e. the author remains vested even after the license is granted or the transfer is completed.

Finally, for payment the law lays down the following basic principles. If the parties have established term of payment those shall be considered the final determination between the parties and the provisions contained therein shall be obviously respected. In absence of such provisions, the right holder/and or any user shall pay remuneration to the author(s) pursuant to the standards for payment of remuneration formulated by the copyright administrative authorities of the State Council jointly with the other relevant authorities.

4.8 Infringement

Commonly Copyright infringement is defined as "*the violation, piracy or theft of a copyright holder's rights through the unauthorized use of a copyrighted work*". The Chinese legal framework identifies different violations against which different provisions apply. Firstly, the law specifically provides that individual or entity who have committed the following infringement acts shall bear civil liability to stop infringement, eliminate impact, apologise, and compensate losses in accordance with the circumstances:

(i) Publication of a work without the consent of the copyrights' holder;
(ii) Publication of a work jointly created with others as a personal independently created work without the consent of the co-author(s);
(iii) Passing off as author of others' work without participating in the creation of the work to seek personal fame and fortune;
(iv) Distortion of or tampering with others' work;
(v) Plagiarism of others' work;
(vi) Use of a work in the form of exhibition, film making and any other methods similar to film making without the consent of the copyright holder, or use of a work in the form of adaptation, translation, annotation, etc., unless otherwise stipulated in this Law;
(vii) Failure to pay remuneration which should have paid for use of others' work;
(viii) Lease of a film work or a work created using methods similar to film making or computer software or audio-visual recordings without the consent of the copyright holder of such works or the holder of copyright-related rights, unless otherwise stipulated in this Law;
(ix) Use of the layout design of a book or a periodical without the consent of the book publisher or periodical publisher;
(x) Live broadcast or public transmission of a live performance or recording of the performance without the consent of the performers; and
(xi) Any other acts which infringe upon copyright and copyright-related rights and interests.

The law identifies different set of violations, various types of copyrights infringements where liability as introduced above it is not the sole protection against such acts. In fact, whereas the nature of the infringement involves more economical aspects of the copyrights the related malicious acts are further censored, additional measures are available jointly with specific retribution and punishment. As for instance confiscation of legal income and/or of the counterfeited material (and subsequent destruction) may be ordered, as well as administrative fines may be imposed. Moreover, whereas the act is deemed sufficiently serious, the confiscation and the destruction of tools, materials and equipment used to create the counterfeit goods (i.e. notably confiscation and destruction of moulds, models, drawings, even machinery) may be ordered. Finally, whereas an act shall also constitute a criminal offence as defined by the relevant criminal laws, the related criminal liability for such acts shall be also pursued in accordance with the same law.

In consideration of the above, Copyright law classifies certain acts worth of enhanced protection and states as follow (Article 48) "*Persons who have committed the following infringement acts shall bear civil liability to stop infringement, eliminate impact, apologise, compensate losses,* etc. *in accordance with the circumstances; where public interest is also compromised, the copyright administrative authorities may order the offender to stop infringement acts, confiscate illegal income, confiscate and destroy infringing replicas, and may impose a fine; where the case is serious, the copyright administrative authorities may also confiscate the materials, tools, equipment,* etc. *mainly used for production of the infringing replicas; where the case constitutes a criminal offence, criminal liability shall be pursued in accordance with the law*"

The same Article 48 enlists the related infringement acts as follows:

(i) Reproduction, distribution, performance, screening, broadcasting, compilation or transmission of others' works to the public through information network without the consent of the copyright holder, unless otherwise stipulated in this Law;
(ii) Publication of books for which another party has exclusive publication rights;
(iii) Reproduction or distribution of audio-visual recordings of a performance or transmission of the performance to the public through information network without the consent of the performers, unless otherwise stipulated in this Law;
(iv) Reproduction or distribution of audio-visual recordings or transmission of audio-visual recordings to the public through information network without the consent of the producers of audio-visual recordings, unless otherwise stipulated in this Law;
(v) Broadcast or reproduction of radio and television programmes without the consent, unless otherwise stipulated in this Law;
(vi) Intentional circumvention or sabotage of the technical measures adopted by rights holders for protection of the copyright or copyright-related rights of their works, audio-visual recordings, etc. without the consent of the copyright holder or the holder of copyright-related rights, unless otherwise stipulated by laws and administrative regulations;
(vii) Intentional deletion or alteration of electronic data for rights management of works, audio-visual recordings, etc. without the consent of the copyright holder or the holder of copyright-related rights, unless otherwise stipulated by laws and administrative regulations; and
(viii) Passing off others' works and production or sale of such works.

The following article express a principle regarding the determination of the amount of compensation, which is recurrent in the Chinese legal framework of intellectual property protection, other than in copyright protection, the same might be found for instance (not exclusively but also) within the provisions of Trademark Law of PRC, Patent Law of the PRC and finally in the Anti-Unfair Competition Law of the PRC. These provision all follow the same principle with some variations in the actual threshold.

According to this principle, the determination of the amount of compensation to be recognised in favour of the holder shall take into account the 'actual losses' as suffered by the rightful owner of the copyright. The same principle for liquidation states that the compensation liquidated by the Court (or the Arbitration Court) whenever difficult to be determined in such manner, alternatively shall be based on the illegal income gained by the infringer during the perpetration of the act. The same determination finally, shall also include "reasonable" expenses incurred by the rightful holder of the copyright in order to stop such act. This legal framework as set out, begs to several considerations.

Firstly, the principle of actual losses makes difficult to obtain an actual and satisfactory amount of compensation whereas the investigation and/or the collection of evidence is not properly and carefully conducted. Therefore, the victim of infringement has to start in advance to collect evidence of any loss. Therefore, in order to obtain a successful result, it become of the utmost importance to preserve and to build evidence against the infringer in order to maximise the amount of damages to be liquidated. Entrusting a professional and seek for legal assistance months after the acts are consumed and damage are suffered might be too late or might anyway jeopardize the possibility to obtain a favourable judgment. In practice it is statistically easier to prove such acts of infringement, not always to obtain a proportionate or sufficient compensation related to the same.

Secondly, regarding the provided alternative to be able to prove the illegal gains we shall further note that, whilst in dispute of (e.g.) unfair competition or dispute among companies that legally conduct their businesses in doing so with their acts violate the law or damage other parties, it fairly easier to collect data such as one company's turnover, or the specific income of one particular individual, or again to represent in Court a deal as concluded or track down a personal gain, as well as some misappropriation of funds. On the contrary, whenever dealing with counterfeiters, the same evidence might be comparatively much harder to prove or even collect. It is in fact harder to prove such 'illegitimate income' and particularly the exact amount. The illegitimate income of the infringer may be difficult, if not impossible, to trace back and to prove in its amount, as reported before, even when the act or the circumstance itself is fairly easy to be proven, it might be hard to delimit the related amount. Same difficulties might be encountered in collecting evidences against an infringer and to prove the actual amount of its illegal gains, whenever such infringer operates illegitimately, perhaps in absence of proper business license and/or business address, and/or manages transactions largely with cash payments (or conducts business manly sheltered overseas). If not proper action are taken in advance, such as due diligence on its business entities and unit, notarization of evidence, request of Court support or injunctions, even large amount of income might be appear much more shirked in the eyes of the Court.

Separately, foreign operators shall consider also that, in China, the concept of "reasonable" expenses as incurred in order to stop the infringement to be included in the final compensation amount not necessarily represent all the legal expenses as we might understand it some western legal framework. Local notary expenses to notarize evidence, as well as the legal assistance costs, might be included in the applicant request to the Court, it is the Judge however that liquidate a certain amount for the expenses and this will be refunded to the applicant. Partial cost of investigation (especially in complex cases where the abovementioned procedure and collection might be very expensive in term of time and resources). Even if might not be fully refunded as "reasonable costs" it may yet increase dramatically the amount of compensation eventually liquidated whenever the same activity would be functional to prove amount of sales or perhaps the illegal income of the defendant (for e.g.). Same for legal cost and expenses, the total amount of legal fees might not be entirely—most commonly partially—recognized by the Court and due by party against which the judgment is rendered.

Finally, whereas determination is impossible using any of the criteria listed above the same provision (as in the other IP laws cited above) specifies that "People's Court" shall rule on compensation of no more that RMB 500,000 in accordance with the extent (and the nature) of the infringement act.

Therefore a threshold exists and up to that sum the related liquidation can always be claimed whenever an act of infringement is proven or recognized by the Court, but the actual amount of losses suffered by the rightful holder or illegitimate income of the infringer are not determinable (recently upgraded up to 500,000 also in other laws such as Anti-unfair Competition Law and Trademark Law, in November 2019). Nonetheless the same amount must be liquidated by the Court, which retains the power of granting such amount based only on the nature of the infringement. This leaves plenty of room of free determination for the Judge called to make this decision.

In practice the fixed amount is rarely entirely liquidated. In these cases, compensation tend not to exceed 80% of the amount expressed above. Thresholds were upgraded recently (on average have been for no more than RMB 300,000 for many years) also in consideration of the fact that, in practice often both requirements above are difficult to fulfil. Therefore if the infringement cases are not properly managed for the occurrence of such acts and damages, commonly compensation is liquidated in consideration of a portion of the fixed amount, mainly based upon the mere perception of the Court over the nature and severity ("the extent") of the same infringement. These events occur especially where protection was activated in a slow or not efficient manner. In consideration of the above, victim of infringement shall act promptly and in a very efficient manner not only to immediately stop the act and contain damages but also to secure future evidence in order to obtain more adequate compensation (whether it is a trademark, patent or copyright infringement).

In term of infringement and related liability special rules finally apply in case of online infringements.

Within this field most important rules are set forth by the Measures for administrative protection of Internet Copyright (2005) which imposes—under certain circumstances—liability on internet service providers and information providers, especially in the form of administrative penalties.

Within the Chinese legal system since 2001, any conduct related to making available or accessible any copyrighted work online unauthorized it constitute an act of infringement.

Network service provider or NSP, enjoys anyway a "safe harbour" mechanism to contain their liability if they satisfy certain compliance requirement in providing their ordinary services. In case that the exemption is not applicable, or requirement are not met, they shall be considered liable for "*knowingly or willingly diffuse, upload, maintain, distribute or supply circumvention methods, devices or materials*". Among the obligations imposed to the NSPs there are the active monitoring, prompt removal, connection block of infringing content upon request of the copyright holder and/or his/her agent in PRC, upon holder's request notice whereas no action is taken within a given time frame (normally 60 days), joint liability mostly in the form of administrative fines shall apply.

4.9 Enforcement

Enforcement of copyrights may be activated in two different level, judicial and administrative, the first however do not exclude the latter. Furthermore, as it is for the related registration, among administrative enforcement, software disputes are regulated separately. Finally, criminal liability may jointly apply to civil liability subject to certain conditions explained below.

Civil litigation and court actions are by far the most advisable to be activated unless the actual circumstances indicate that would be hard or very difficult to enforce the obtained judgment against the defendant, i.e. the same is untraceable (this apply mainly with online violations and where is hard to track or find a liable subject, or other practical enforcement issues may present) or again, even if traceable the subject either individual or company (legitimate or otherwise) do not present sufficient asset at its disposal.

Court remedies become more convenient since the start of the 2000s when statutory damages and most importantly preliminary injunctions were introduced. In addition, shall be noted that in practice civil remedies are applicable in a more extended range of cases, where on the contrary administrative injunction, fines and remedies are available only against straightforward violations. Furthermore, in case both remedies administrative and judicial are to be requested, timing of request and order in the request may play a vital role, therefore the timing of activation of the same remedies shall be carefully evaluated in advance. In collecting the evidence for instance, investigation very often requires the defendant unaware collaboration, and that would be impossible to achieve after injunction request or report to the authorities is made.

Under PRC law and regulation copyright holders and other entitled individual may apply to People's Court for a preliminary injunction against an act of infringement and for property and/or evidence preservation orders. The requestor shall present evidence to the Court that indicates that (a) another person is actively violating a copyright and/or imminently will do the same; (b) delay in forcibly ceasing the act will (almost) irreparably damage the applicant of the remedy. In addition, shall be noted that "Damage" by case law, include those attaining to the author's reputation and name rather than only economical losses.

As it is for trademark, other than Court order to merely stop the infringement, upon conditions as above, the applicant may request also the preservation of evidence. In case, the Court shall provide its opinion and issue the related order within 48 h from the application. In granting the measure the Court will order the applicant to pay a security deposit proportional to the value of sized goods. Preservation measures are issued without hearing or summon of the defendant. Security will be retained by the Court, whereas further in the proceeding, evidence provided to the Court by the claimant will be found void, mendacious or anyway successfully discredited. Article

51 of Copyright law regarding preservation of evidence specifies that in case security is requested but not timely provided, the request of preservation shall be denied.

Moreover, the same article provides that if no proceeding is started within 15 days from the adoption of the above-mentioned measures the Court's order shall be lifted.

For sake of simplicity the pre-emptive measures are regulated directly by the same law instrument providing for other intellectual property rights, of which the validity shall apply also to copyrights by express will of the Supreme People's Court of PRC. As decided, the provisions contained in the interpretations pertaining the preservation of evidence and the right of exclusive use of Trademark regulate also copyright issues jointly with relevant articles of Civil Procedural law of PRC (e.g. 93, 96 and 99 as recalled by article 50 of Copyright law).

For trials, as examined before, liability shall be borne by the distributor, seller, displayer or the user (as defined by the relevant paragraphs above) whereas the same is unable to prove the authorization of the author to perform such acts. Therefore, in case of supposed violations of the rights as defined in detail by the law (paragraph 8 above) the infringer is challenged to prove the rightful authorization to avoid liability.

As per Article 54, liability raises also whereas a party was bond to perform contractual obligations or the same obligations do not satisfy the agreed criteria, recalling contractual liability (descending from Contract Law of the PRC and General Principle of the Civil Law of the People's Republic of China).

As per dispute resolution forum, as specifically provided by the law a copyright disputes may be settled by mediation or may be submitted to an arbitration agency (to be read as "commission") for arbitration, pursuant to arbitration agreement:

(a) concluded between the involved parties; or
(b) contained in the copyright contract. Where one of the two condition is not met—law specify that—the parties may file a lawsuit directly with People's Court (Article 55 Copyright law).

In addition to what is provided by Article 55 as just quoted, that validity of any arbitration agreement and/or clause it is regulated by the Arbitration law of the People Republic of China, and written arbitration clause between the party it is only one of the different mandatory requirement, which also include (for instance) the designation by the arbitration clause of an arbitration commission and scope of dispute to be resolved. Therefore, the relevant part of the agreement between the parties or "the clause in the Copyright contract" shall be drafted accordingly or it shall be considered void.

Administrative enforcement, as introduced above, it is recognized for literary, artistic, design and related works, as well as, software (and related works), yet with some differences in the two main categories.

Copyright owners may (directly or assisted by an agent) file complains within the administrative body for copyright infringement. Bureaus of Culture, Broadcasting Media and TV (wording may present minor differences within local bureaus).

Authorities are entitled to exercise the following rage of powers pertaining to:

(i) Cease the infringement;
(ii) Size of evidences/evidence preservation measures;
(iii) Confiscation of illegal income, reproductions, counterfeit goods;
(iv) Order destruction of the counterfeit goods;
(v) Under certain circumstances order seizure and destruction of tools and equipment used to carry out such infringements.
(vi) Commend fines to the infringer.

The method of determination of fines works similarly to the liquidation of compensation in Court, regulated by Copyright implementing regulations 2013. Fines are linked to the stream and amount of revenue of the infringer. Where no determination is possible, fine may be imposed up to RMB 250,000. On the contrary whereas possible to determine illegal income or revenue of the infringer, fine may be imposed up to five times the total amount of illegit transactions.

Software regulations provides very similar powers, in "serious" cases or violations, however authorities may confiscate (and destroy) tools, equipment (common to non-software rules) and *facilities* involved in the process of infringement of the software copyright. Fines are determined over certain acts, considered to be particularly offensive or dangerous, and linked to the value of the counterfeited or better—illegally distributed—goods. Whenever the infringement involves the evasion and destruction of informatic prevention and protection measures in place to avoid the same act of infringement (e.g. violation via hacking activities, voluntary circumvention, evasion and/or destruction of any anti-circumvention systems and measures) a fine up to RMB 200,000 may be imposed. Notwithstanding a fine of RMB 100/each piece sold, distributed or anyway made available could be imposed by the authorities. Jointly or alternatively depending on the actual circumstances a fine proportional to the value of the goods may be imposed up to five time the value. Determination of such value is left entirely to the authorities do determine, in consideration of the fact that laws and regulations are silent in this regard.

Authorities are not entitled to liquidate any compensation for damage suffered by the vested owner.

Therefore, lawsuit shall be considered in advance, especially after a positive result of due diligence on infringer's assets.

On this regard, since some action may be alternatively requested also to the Court, timing, manner and—most importantly—opportunity to apply for same and/or similar measures also via the administrative bodies as well shall be evaluated. Mainly circumstances regarding likelihood of future lawsuits, location and secrecy shall be carefully considered. If no action in Court it is foreseeable in the near future, then request for administrative actions shall always be made. As for location, while most of the main cities, tier 1 and 2 cities are to be considered very or anyway rather safe in term of local protectionism, some problem may arise in very remote areas, where authorities may still wish to protect local interests. In this case problem may be resolved with (a) report to a higher body (may take long) or more advisable (b) consider bypassing local administrative measures and request judicial measures instead.

In practice, court are fairly more distant from the infringer's location and its sphere of influence. As per secrecy as said, a too fast involvement of authorities which will start their own investigation, may seize evidence, order to cease activities, impose fines, will surely put the infringer(s) in a higher state of alert and jeopardize the right holder's evidence collection activities.

Chapter 5
IP Rights Protection and Enforcement in Other Provisions

5.1 Trade Secrets (Anti-unfair Competition)

Trade secret are that information that are not generally known to the public, their secrecy confer economic benefit on its holder because the information is not publicly known and for the same reason the holder (a commercial operator) makes reasonable efforts to maintain them undisclosed to third parties.

Trade secrets are an intangible, unregistrable yet very valuable IP right. They are also related to commercial competition in the sense that if disclosed, they represent an advantage for the commercial operator to which the information is disclosed with.

By general definition, trade secrets may be considered all corporate information, regardless of forms, including processes, methods, recipes, specification, business and marketing strategies, customer lists, materials, technical and financial information so long as they meet requirements specified by the law.

Specific Definition of "Trade Secret" and a Delimitation of the Acts of Infringement of the same might be Found in Article 9 of the newly revised Anti-unfair Competition Law of the PRC (2019).

"Commercial secrets referred to in this Law shall mean commercial information such as technical information and business information, which is not known to the public and has commercial value and for which the rights holder has adopted the corresponding confidentiality measures".

The same article 9 follows with definition of the scope of infringement and subjects possibly involved.

Business operators shall not commit the following infringement of commercial secrets:

obtain the commercial secrets of a rights holder through theft,
bribery, fraud, coercion, hacking or other improper means;
disclose, use or allow others to use the commercial secrets of a rights holder obtained through the aforesaid means;

G. Pisacane and D. Zibetti, *Intellectual Property in China*, China Law, Tax & Accounting,
https://doi.org/10.1007/978-981-15-4558-0_5

violate confidentiality obligation or violate a rights holder's requirements on keeping confidentiality of commercial secrets, and disclose, use or allow others to use such commercial secrets they obtained; and

instigate, induce or assist others to violate confidentiality obligation or to violate a rights holder's requirements on keeping confidentiality of commercial secrets, so as to disclose, use or allow others to use the commercial secrets of the rights holder.

The delimitation of possible infringor is wide, stretching from natural persons, legal persons and non-legal persons other than business operators committing any of the illegal acts stipulated above it is deemed to have infringed upon commercial secrets.

Where a third party is knowingly aware or should be aware that an employee, ex-employee of a rights holder of commercial secrets, or any other organisation or individual, has committed any of the illegal acts stipulated in the first paragraph of this Article but still obtains, discloses, uses or allows others to use such commercial secrets, this shall be deemed to have infringed upon commercial secrets.

The newly amended AUCL 2019, represent a great improvement of the accorded protection. In regards of the acts of violation in addition to misappropriation by theft, bribery, fraud, coercion, or other improper means, electronic intrusion/hacking is now specifically named.

The definition of trade secret itself is extended to any kinds of commercial information that qualify as a trade secret if proper measures are taken to protect confidentiality is now protected by the law, which prior the amendment merely included technical or business information. Previous limitations of protection to "business operators" now also includes natural persons, legal persons, and organizations without legal personality.

In term of compensation, as it was highlighted for Trademark and Copyright (as well as for Patent in the newly published draft) the new law increases the threshold for statutory damages, i.e. damages that might be liquidated as last resort in case is not possible to link the same damages are unquantifiable (e.g.) unlawful profit is not proved, the statutory damages are now increase up to RMB 5 million (previously RMB 3 million).

Also, in respect of punitive damages: for malicious misappropriation the amount to be liquidated may be up to fivefold the actual damages suffered by the owner of trade secret, or fivefold of the illicit gains of the defendant.

Furthermore, the burden of proof it has been modified, now lays upon the infringor. Previously, trade secret owners were required to establish: (a) a defendant's access or exposure to the information; and (b) that the information used was substantially the same as the trade secret. After new modifications and according to the similar principle as provided for trademark infringement—the defendant has only the obligation to provide prima facie evidence of having implemented (i.e. set forth, provided) confidentiality measures and reasonably demonstrate that the trade secret has been anyway misused or misappropriated. The burden then shifts to the defendant to prove that the asserted trade secret is not one protected by the law.

The burden also shifts to the defendant (to disprove that misappropriation exists) if the owner provides preliminary evidence reasonably demonstrating that the trade secret has been misappropriated, and provides evidence of one of the following evidences indicating that the defendant has:

(i) means or opportunity to obtain the trade secret, and that the information used is substantially identical to the trade secret;
(ii) divulged, disclosed or anyway used trade secrets, or there is the risk that the same actions are imminent;
(iii) provided other evidence indicating misuse or misappropriation of a trade secret.

5.2 Foreign Investment Law (2019)

IP protection is further regulated for the related aspects by the Foreign Investment Law of the People's Republic of China (2019) "FIL".

The law as adopted March 15, 2019, it is set to come into force on January 1, 2020.

The law abrogates three existing laws on foreign investments within the territory of the People's Republic of China: i.e. Chinese-foreign equity joint ventures law EJV, wholly foreign-owned enterprises law WFOE, and Chinese-foreign contractual joint ventures CJV, with the scope of unifying the related provisions.

This law was implemented during the "trade war" negotiation, representing also a reasonable response to US allegations regarding Intellectual property theft and forced technology transfer; abuse of office positions and related powers by the authorities; de facto mandatory partnership with local companies for foreigners in venturing in certain sectors (negative list), subsidies given to local firms and for now not accessible to foreign companies as established in the territory.

The new legal framework as outlined in the new Foreign Investment Law which is likely to be implemented by several different regulation, carry the following principles:

(i) prohibit forced tech transfers sanctioning related acts of administrative bodies which may harm the same rights.
(ii) calls for more equality and fairness in the field for tech imports to China;
(iii) enhance trade secret protection, portending for increased protection of foreign IP rights being transferred/licensed into China, whether as a consequence of cross-border licensing arrangement or a foreign investment within the territory.

The Foreign Investment Law emphasises that FIEs' and their foreign owners' intellectual property shall be protected and encourages voluntary technical cooperation. It specifically prohibits PRC administrative authorities from using administrative measures to coerce an FIE into transferring technology or from divulging confidential information or trade secrets of the FIE and foreign investors. FIL requires administrative authorities to maintain the same as confidential and provides for sanctions for unauthorized and unlawful disclosures.

On this respect the law states: *Administrative authorities and their working personnel shall keep confidential, in accordance with the law, the trade secrets of foreign investors and foreign-invested enterprises to which they are privy in the course of performing their duties, and may not disclose or illegally provide the same to third parties.*

And again on the same topic (article 39) *If a member of the working personnel of an administrative authority abuses its authority, neglecting its duties, practices favouritism, commits another irregularity or discloses or illegally provides trade secrets to which he/she was privy in the course of performing his/her duties to a third party in the course of foreign investment promotion, protection or administration work, he/she shall be disciplined in accordance with the law. If a criminal offense is constituted, his/her criminal liability shall be pursued in accordance with the law.*

The Foreign investment law is not the only law prescribing how administrative authorities should act with respect to trade secrets, or generally in regards of intellectual property rights. Similar provision are to be found (including but not limited to) in Anti Unfair Competition law, in the Patent law and Custom Regulations (as better analysed below) all prescribing civil and (for serious cases) criminal liabilities for authorities, and staff member that abuse of their powers or position, to infringe, damage or impair protection of Intellectual Property Rights during the performance of their own duties.

5.3 Web Pages "Take Down"

In protecting intellectual property rights, commercial operators shall carefully evaluate case by case benefit and costs—in term of time and resources that might be incurred in instructing a case, collecting evidence and finally handling the matter in Court in several judgments. In the light of the above it may happen that among several violations suffered at the same time, some are worth to be protected via judicial proceedings, some others are to be resolved via administrative protection. Sometimes opportunity to combine protections are to be considered, in any case, even for minor violation, as long as the same are self-evident (to a certain degree) the latter way is almost always advisable (as a last resort).

The present remedy, if activated instantly after violation, in some cases might preclude further evidence gathering and finally jeopardize an eventual judicial procedure. Therefore the proper time to resort to it shall be evaluated as well.

Web pages take down is a tool for commercial operators of administrative granted IP protection which can be used against web pages that displays, with the aim of commercialize, products that illegally use IP rights without consent. The web page can be a website or a single page inside the several e-commerce platforms popular in China such as, Alibaba, Taobao, T-Mall or JD.

According to the AUCL, online platforms are co-responsible for the violation of the intellectual property rights if they do not take down the page and the link even after a notification.

The "Notice and Take Down Action" is the procedure trough the owner of the trademark requires to the online platform to take down the page containing illegal contents.

The major e-commerce platforms in China, adopt their own internal regulations for this kind of procedures.

Usually procedure requires:

(i) proof that the applicant is the legal owner of that intellectual property right (certificate is required);
(ii) internet addresses where the claimed violation are hosted (link);
(iii) Business license of the applicant (agent in China might be required for foreign operators that are not incorporated).

These procedures can be done independently (without representation) by the rights holder when in possession of a regular Business License but ability to operate in Chinese language is required in order to successfully handling the procedure. It is recommended to refer to an expert also to conduct periodic checks to identify the illegal displays. If in one hand the remedy is quick and easy, on the other hand when a web page is taken down, another one can easily pop up with the same content hosted in another link. A constant monitoring and an active approach can demotivate illegal activities, jointly with possible fines pending on the infringor.

5.4 Customs Protection of Intellectual Property Right

Another way to enhance protection against violation on intellectual property rights is the custom protection as set forth by Regulations of PRC on Customs Protection on Intellectual Property Rights (as revised in 2018).

These Regulations are formulated pursuant to the Customs Law of the People's Republic of China for the purposes of enforcing Customs protection of intellectual property rights. Law states clearly (article 3) *Imports and exports that have infringed upon intellectual property rights shall be prohibited by the State.*

Customs protection of intellectual property rights referred to in these Regulations mean the protection implemented by the Customs on the rights to the exclusive use of trademarks, copyrights and copyright-related rights, and patent rights (hereinafter referred to collectively as the "Intellectual Property Rights") in respect of the imports and exports under the protection of the laws and administrative regulations of the People's Republic of China.

The same regulation provides that the Customs "must safeguard Intellectual Property Protection as granted by this regulation and existing laws".

Where the intellectual property rights holders find that the suspected infringing goods are about to be imported or exported, they may apply to the Customs at the port of entry or exit of the goods for detaining such suspected infringing goods.

In these cases, where the intellectual property rights holder requests for Customs detention of the suspected infringing goods, they shall submit an application form, the relevant certification documents and provide evidence that is sufficient to prove the obvious existence of such infringement. Where the intellectual property rights holder requests for Customs detention of the suspected infringing goods, it is required to provide the Customs a guarantee which does not exceed the value of the goods, to be used as compensation against the losses caused to the import agent, consignor or consignee due to the improper application, and as the fees for warehousing, custody and disposal of goods incurred by the Customs for detention of the goods; where the intellectual property rights holders directly pay the fees for warehousing and custody to the warehouseman, such amount shall be deducted from the guarantee. Authorities have a great discretion in determining such limits regarding deposit.

To proceed it is required to specify the goods involved and submit the related intellectual property rights registration certificate. Once the application is approved by the competent authority (GAC, General Administration of Customs), the customs authorities will take actions accordingly. Moreover, if prior registration is made, the applicant can fully benefit from customs protection. Customs authorities can proceed ex officio against the violation, if occurred, impose penalties and seize the goods. In case each time a violation of filed trademark, patent or copyright registered within the customs is discovered, the Custom will notify the registrant. The same will decide whether to proceed or not against such violation.

Where the detained suspected infringing goods are found to have infringed upon the intellectual property rights upon investigation by the Customs, the Customs shall confiscate such goods.

Upon confiscation of the goods that have infringed upon the intellectual property rights, the Customs shall notify the intellectual property rights holder in writing of the relevant information on such goods.

Whether it is a single application made by the holder or either the authority ex officio, where the confiscated goods that infringe upon the intellectual property rights may be used for social public welfare, the Customs shall transfer such goods to the relevant public welfare organisations for use in social public welfare; where the intellectual property rights holder intends to purchase such goods, the Customs may make a compensated transfer of the goods to the intellectual property rights holder. Where the confiscated goods that infringe upon the intellectual property rights cannot be used for social public welfare and the intellectual property rights holders do not intend to purchase the goods, the Customs may auction off the goods pursuant to the law upon eliminating the infringement characteristics; however, imported counterfeit trademark goods are not allowed to enter into commercial channels by simply removing the trademark labels on the goods, except for special circumstances; where it is impossible to eliminate the infringement characteristics, the Customs shall destroy the goods.

Where the imports or exports infringe upon the intellectual property rights and constitute a criminal offence, criminal liability shall be pursued in accordance with the law.

These alternative measures are effective if combined together with the web site pages take down. In order to plan out the most suitable strategy, implementation shall be evaluated case by case, and an expert opinion on the matter it is advisable.

Chapter 6
Proposed Translation for Trademark Law (November 11, 2019)

Abstract Trademark Law of the People's Republic of China (2019 revision).

中华人民共和国商标法 **(2019 修订)**

Trademark Law of the People's Republic of China (2019 revision)
[translation for reference only]
Authority: National People's Congress Standing Committee
Published: April 23, 2019

Effective: November 11, 2019

G. Pisacane and D. Zibetti, *Intellectual Property in China*, China Law, Tax & Accounting,
https://doi.org/10.1007/978-981-15-4558-0_6

第 一 章 总 则	**Chapter 1 General Principles**
第一条 为了加强商标管理，保护商标专用权，促使生产、经营者保证商品和服务质量，维护商标信誉，以保障消费者和生产、经营者的利益，促进社会主义市场经济的发展，特制定本法。	**Article 1** This Law is formulated for the purposes of strengthening trademark administration, protecting exclusive rights to use trademark, promoting quality assurance for commodities and services by manufacturers and business operators, safeguarding trademark reputation, protecting the interests of consumers, manufacturers and business operators, and promoting development of socialist market economy.
第二条 国务院工商行政管理部门商标局主管全国商标注册和管理的工作。 国务院工商行政管理部门设立商标评审委员会，负责处理商标争议事宜。	**Article 2** The trademark bureau of the administration for industry and commerce department of the State Council shall be in charge of trademark registration and administration nationwide. The administration for industry and commerce department of the State Council shall establish a trademark review and adjudication board to be responsible for handling trademark disputes.
第三条 经商标局核准注册的商标为注册商标，包括商品商标、服务商标和集体商标、证明商标；商标注册人	**Article 3** Trademarks approved and registered by the

享有商标专用权，受法律保护。 本法所称集体商标，是指以团体、协会或者其他组织名义注册，供该组织成员在商事活动中使用，以表明使用者在该组织中的成员资格的标志。 本法所称证明商标，是指由对某种商品或者服务具有监督能力的组织所控制，而由该组织以外的单位或者个人使用于其商品或者服务，用以证明该商品或者服务的原产地、原料、制造方法、质量或者其他特定品质的标志。 集体商标、证明商标注册和管理的特殊事项，由国务院工商行政管理部门规定。	trademark bureaux are registered trademarks, including commodity trademarks, service marks and collective trademarks, certification marks; trademark registrants enjoy exclusive rights to use trademark and are protected by the law. A collective trademark referred to in this Law shall mean a mark registered in the name of a group, association or any other organisation to be used by the organisation's members in commercial activities and to indicate a user's membership in the said organisation. A certification mark referred to in this Law shall mean a mark controlled by an organisation which has supervisory capacity over certain commodities or services to be used by organisations or individuals other than the said organisation on their commodities or services to prove the place of origin, raw materials, manufacturing method, quality or other specific quality of the said commodities or services. Specific matters pertaining to registration and administration of collective trademarks and certification marks shall be stipulated by the administration for industry and commerce department of the State Council.
第四条 自然人、法人或者其他组织在生产经营活动中，对其商品或者服务需要取得商标专用权的，应当向商标局申请商标注册。不以使用为目的的恶意商标注册申请，应当予以驳回。 本法有关商品商标的规定，适用于服务商标。	**Article 4** Natural persons, legal persons or any other organisations that need to obtain exclusive rights to use trademark for their commodities or services in the course of their manufacturing and business activities shall apply to a trademark bureau for trademark registration. Any application for trademark registration that is malicious and is not filed for the purpose of use shall be rejected. The provisions of this Law on trademarks for commodities shall apply to service marks
第五条 两个以上的自然人、法人或者其他组织可以共同向商标局申请注册同一商标，共同享有和行使该商标专用权。	**Article 5** Two or more natural persons, legal persons or any other organisations may jointly apply to a trademark
第六条 法律、行政法规规定必须使用注册商标的商品，必须申请商标注册，未经核准注册的，不得在市场销售。	

	bureau for registration of the same trademark to jointly enjoy and exercise exclusive rights to use the said trademark.
	Article 6 Commodities for which the use of registered trademark is stipulated by laws and administrative regulations shall apply for trademark registration, the commodities shall not be sold in the market prior to approval and registration.
第七条 申请注册和使用商标，应当遵循诚实信用原则。 商标使用人应当对其使用商标的商品质量负责。各级工商行政管理部门应当通过商标管理，制止欺骗消费者的行为。	**Article 7** Application for registration and use of trademarks shall comply with the principles of honesty and trustworthiness. Trademark users shall be responsible for the quality of the commodities which use the trademark. All levels of administration for industry and commerce shall curb consumer fraud activities through trademark administration.
第八条 任何能够将自然人、法人或者其他组织的商品与他人的商品区别开的标志，包括文字、图形、字母、数字、三维标志、颜色组合和声音等，以及上述要素的组合，均可以作为商标申请注册。	**Article 8** Any mark which can differentiate the commodities of a natural person, legal person or any other organisation with the commodities of others, including text, graphics, alphabets, numbers, three-dimensional mark, colour combination and sound, etc, and a combination of the aforesaid elements, may be registered as a trademark.
第九条 申请注册的商标，应当有显著特征，便于识别，并不得与他人在先取得的合法权利相冲突。 商标注册人有权标明"注册商标"或者注册标记。	**Article 9** A trademark to be registered shall possess distinctive characteristics to facilitate identification and shall not conflict with prior legitimate rights obtained by others. Trademark registrants shall have the right to state the wordings "registered trademark" or the registered mark.
第十条 下列标志不得作为商标使用： (一)同中华人民共和国的国家名称、国旗、国徽、国歌、军旗、军徽、军歌、勋章等相同或者近似的，以及同中央国家机关的名称、标志、所在地特定地点的名称或者标志性建筑物的名称、图形相同的； (二)同外国的国家名称、国旗、国徽、军旗等相同或者近似的，但经该国政府同意的除外； (三)同政府间国际组织的名称、旗帜、徽记等相同或	**Article 10** The following marks shall not be used as a

者近似的，但经该组织同意或者不易误导公众的除外； (四)与表明实施控制、予以保证的官方标志、检验印记相同或者近似的，但经授权的除外； (五)同"红十字"、"红新月"的名称、标志相同或者近似的； (六)带有民族歧视性的； (七)带有欺骗性，容易使公众对商品的质量等特点或者产地产生误认的； (八)有害于社会主义道德风尚或者有其他不良影响的。	trademark: (1) a mark identical or similar to the country name, national flag, national emblem, national anthem, military flag, military emblem, military anthem, military medal, etc of the People's Republic of China, and a mark identical to the name and logo of Central government agencies, name of the specific location where it is located or name or figure of landmark building; (2) a mark identical or similar to the country name, national flag, national emblem, military flag of a foreign country, except with the consent of the said government; (3) a mark identical or similar to the name, flag, emblem of an international inter-governmental organisation, except with the consent of the said organisation or where the public is unlikely to be misled; (4) a mark identical or similar to an official logo or hallmark which indicates control or assurance, except where duly authorised (5) a mark identical or similar to the name or logo of "red cross", "red crescent"; (6) a mark which is racially discriminatory; (7) a mark which is deceptive, easy to cause the public to be misled over the characteristics such as quality or place of origin of commodities; or (8) a mark which is detrimental to socialist morals or has any other adverse impact.
县级以上行政区划的地名或者公众知晓的外国地名，不得作为商标。但是，地名具有其他含义或者作为集体商标、证明商标组成部分的除外；已经注册的使用地名的商标继续有效。	Geographical names of administrative regions of county level and above or overseas geographical names well known by the public shall not be used as trademarks, except where a geographical name has any other meaning or where it is an integral part of a collective trademark or certification mark; trademarks bearing a geographical name which have been registered shall continue to be valid.
第十一条 下列标志不得作为商标注册： (一)仅有本商品的通用名称、图形、型号的； (二)仅直接表示商品的质量、主要原料、功能、用途、重量、数量及其他特点的； (三)其他缺乏显著特征的。 前款所列标志经过使用取得显著特征，并便于识别的，可以作为商标注册。	**Article 11** The following marks shall not be registered as a trademark:

	(1) a mark which merely states the generic name, figure or model number of the commodities; (2) a mark which merely directly expresses the quality, key ingredients, functions, purposes, weight, quantity and other characteristics of the commodities; or (3) a mark which lacks salient features. Where a mark mentioned in the preceding paragraph possesses salient features after use which can facilitate identification, it can be registered as a trademark.
第十二条 以三维标志申请注册商标的，仅由商品自身的性质产生的形状、为获得技术效果而需有的商品形状或者使商品具有实质性价值的形状，不得注册。	**Article 12** A three-dimensional mark which is merely a shape arising from the characteristics of the commodities or a shape of commodities required to obtain technical results or a shape which gives the commodities substantial value shall not be registered.
第十三条 为相关公众所熟知的商标，持有人认为其权利受到侵害时，可以依照本法规定请求驰名商标保护。 就相同或者类似商品申请注册的商标是复制、摹仿或者翻译他人未在中国注册的驰名商标，容易导致混淆的，不予注册并禁止使用。 就不相同或者不相类似商品申请注册的商标是复制、摹仿或者翻译他人已经在中国注册的驰名商标，误导公众，致使该驰名商标注册人的利益可能受到损害的，不予注册并禁止使用。	**Article 13** Where the holder of a trademark which is well known by the relevant public is of the view that its rights are infringed upon, it may request for protection of well-known trademark pursuant to the provisions of this Law. An application for registration of a trademark which is a replication, imitation or translation of other's well-known trademark not registered in China for use on identical or similar commodities which is easily misleading shall not be registered and the use of such a mark shall be prohibited. An application for registration of a trademark which is a replication, imitation or translation of other's well-known trademark already registered in China for use on non-identical or non-similar commodities which is misleading to the public and may cause harm to the interests of the trademark registrant of the said well-known trademark shall not be registered and the use of such a mark shall be prohibited.
第十四条 驰名商标应当根据当事人的请求，作为处理涉及商标案件需要认定的事实进行认定。认定驰名商标应当考虑下列因素： （一）相关公众对该商标的知晓程度； （二）该商标使用的持续时间； （三）该商标的任何宣传工作的持续时间、程度和地理	

范围； (四)该商标作为驰名商标受保护的记录； (五)该商标驰名的其他因素。 在商标注册审查、工商行政管理部门查处商标违法案件过程中，当事人依照本法第十三条规定主张权利的，商标局根据审查、处理案件的需要，可以对商标驰名情况作出认定。 在商标争议处理过程中，当事人依照本法第十三条规定主张权利的，商标评审委员会根据处理案件的需要，可以对商标驰名情况作出认定。 在商标民事、行政案件审理过程中，当事人依照本法第十三条规定主张权利的，最高人民法院指定的人民法院根据审理案件的需要，可以对商标驰名情况作出认定。 生产、经营者不得将"驰名商标"字样用于商品、商品包装或者容器上，或者用于广告宣传、展览以及其他商业活动中。 **第十五条** 未经授权，代理人或者代表人以自己的名义将被代理人或者被代表人的商标进行注册，被代理人或者被代表人提出异议的，不予注册并禁止使用。 就同一种商品或者类似商品申请注册的商标与他人在先使用的未注册商标相同或者近似，申请人与该他	**Article 14** Well-known trademarks shall be ascertained pursuant to the request of the party concerned for the purpose of ascertaining facts for handling of trademark cases. Ascertainment of a well-known trademark shall take into accounts the following factors: (1) the extent of the relevant public's familiarity with the said trademark; (2) the duration of continued use of the said trademark; (3) the duration, extent and geographical scope of any promotional campaign for the said trademark; (4) the record of the said trademark being protected as a well-known trademark; and (5) any other factors for the said trademark's fame. In the course of examination of trademark registration and handling of trademark-related illegal cases by the administration for industry and commerce, where a party concerned asserts its rights pursuant to the provisions of Article 13 of this Law, the trademark bureau may ascertain a well-known trademark based on the needs of examination and handling of the case. In the course of handling trademark disputes, where a party concerned asserts its rights pursuant to the provisions of Article 13 of this Law, the trademark review and adjudication board may ascertain a well-known trademark based on the needs of handling the case. In the course of trial of trademark-related civil and administrative cases, where a party concerned asserts its rights pursuant to the provisions of Article 13 of this Law, a People's Court designated by the Supreme People's Court may ascertain a well-known trademark based on the needs of trying the case. Manufacturers and business operators shall not state the wordings "well-known trademarks" on

人具有前款规定以外的合同、业务往来关系或者其他关系而明知该他人商标存在，该他人提出异议的，不予注册。	commodities, commodity packaging or containers, or use the wordings in advertisements, promotions, exhibitions and other commercial activities. **Article 15** Where an agent or a representative register the trademark of its principal in its own name without authorisation, and the entrusting party raises an objection, the trademark shall not be registered and the use of such a trademark shall be prohibited. For an application for registration of a trademark which is identical or similar to a unregistered trademark which has been used by another person for use on the same type of commodities or similar commodities, where the applicant is aware of the existence of the trademark due to contractual or business relationship or any other relationship with such person other than those stipulated in the preceding paragraph, and such person has raised an objection, the application shall not be approved.
第十六条 商标中有商品的地理标志，而该商品并非来源于该标志所标示的地区，误导公众的，不予注册并禁止使用；但是，已经善意取得注册的继续有效。 前款所称地理标志，是指标示某商品来源于某地区，该商品的特定质量、信誉或者其他特征，主要由该地区的自然因素或者人文因素所决定的标志。	**Article 16** Where a trademark contains a geographical mark of the commodities, and the commodities are not sourced from the regions indicated by the said mark, thus misleading the public, the trademark shall not be registered and the use of such a trademark shall be prohibited, however, trademarks registered previously in good faith shall continue to be valid. A geographical mark referred to in the preceding paragraph shall mean a mark which indicates that certain commodities are sourced from certain regions and in which the specific quality, reputation or any other characteristics of the said commodities is mainly decided by the natural factors or human factors of the said region.
第十七条 外国人或者外国企业在中国申请商标注册的，应当按其所属国和中华人民共和国签订的协议或者共同参加的国际条约办理，或者按对等原则办理。	**Article 17** Applications for trademark registration by foreigners or foreign enterprises in China shall be handled
第十八条 申请商标注册或者办理其他商标事宜，可以自行办理，也可以委托依法设立的商标代理机构办理。 外国人或者外国企业在中国申请商标注册和办理其他商标事宜的，应当委托依法设立的商标代理机构办理。	

第十九条 商标代理机构知道或者应当知道委托人申请注册的商标属于本法第四条、第十五条和第三十二条规定情形的，不得接受其委托。 委托人申请注册的商标可能存在本法规定不得注册情形的，商标代理机构应当明确告知委托人。 商标代理机构知道或者应当知道委托人申请注册的商标属于本法第十五条和第三十二条规定情形的，不得接受其委托。 商标代理机构除对其代理服务申请商标注册外，不得申请注册其他商标。 **第二十条** 商标代理行业组织应当按照章程规定，严格执行吸纳会员的条件，对违反行业自律规范的会员实行惩戒。商标代理行业组织对其吸纳的会员和对会员的惩戒情况，应当及时向社会公布。 **第二十一条** 商标国际注册遵循中华人民共和国缔结或者参加的有关国际条约确立的制度，具体办法由国务院规定。	pursuant to the agreement executed between their country and the People's Republic of China or the international treaty to which their country and the People's Republic of China are participants, or pursuant to the principle of reciprocity. **Article 18** Applicants for trademark registration or any other trademark matters may handle the matter personally or entrust a trademark agency established pursuant to the law to handle the matter. Foreigners or foreign enterprises applying for trademark registration in China and handling any other trademark matters shall entrust a trademark agency established pursuant to the law to handle the matter. **Article 19** Trademark agencies shall comply with the principle of honesty and trustworthiness, comply with laws and administrative regulations, handle trademark registration applications or any other trademark matters in accordance with the entrustment by the entrusting party; keep confidentiality of the entrusting party's commercial secrets which have come into its knowledge in the course of acting as an agent. Where the trademark to be registered by the entrusting party may fall under the scope stipulated by this Law in which registration is not allowed, the trademark agency shall notify the entrusting party clearly. Where a trademark agency is or should be aware that the trademark to be registered by the entrusting party falls under the circumstances stipulated in Article 4, 15 or 32 of this Law, it shall not accept the entrustment. The trademark agency shall not apply for registration of any trademark other than the trademark as entrusted for registration.

第二章 商标注册的申请	**Article 20** Trademark agency industry organisations shall implement their member admission criteria stringently pursuant to the provisions of their articles of association and impose punishment on members who have violated the industry self-discipline norms. Trademark agency industry organisations shall promptly announce information pertaining to admission of members and punishment imposed on their members.
第二十二条 商标注册申请人应当按规定的商品分类表填报使用商标的商品类别和商品名称，提出注册申请。 商标注册申请人可以通过一份申请就多个类别的商品申请注册同一商标。 商标注册申请等有关文件，可以以书面方式或者数据电文方式提出。	**Article 21** International registration of trademarks shall comply with the system established by the relevant international treaty to which the People's Republic of China has concluded or acceded, the detailed measures shall be stipulated by the State Council.
第二十三条 注册商标需要在核定使用范围之外的商品上取得商标专用权的，应当另行提出注册申请。	**Chapter 2 Trademark Registration Applications**
第二十四条 注册商标需要改变其标志的，应当重新提出注册申请。	**Article 22** Applicants for trademark registration shall fill in the category and name of the commodities for which the trademark is used pursuant to the stipulated classification of commodities for the registration application. Applicants for trademark registration may apply for registration of the same trademark through one application for commodities of various categories. Trademark registration application documents may be submitted in hard copy or soft copy.
第二十五条 商标注册申请人自其商标在外国第一次提出商标注册申请之日起六个月内，又在中国就相同商品以同一商标提出商标注册申请的，依照该外国同中国签订的协议或者共同参加的国际条约，或者按照相互承认优先权的原则，可以享有优先权。 依照前款要求优先权的，应当在提出商标注册申请的	**Article 23** Where it is necessary to obtain exclusive rights to use trademark for use of a registered trademark on

时候提出书面声明，并且在三个月内提交第一次提出的商标注册申请文件的副本；未提出书面声明或者逾期未提交商标注册申请文件副本的，视为未要求优先权。	commodities beyond the approved scope of use, a separate registration application shall be submitted. **Article 24** Where there is a need to change a registered trademark, a new registration application shall be submitted. **Article 25** Where an applicant for trademark registration submits a trademark registration application in China for the same trademark for identical commodities within six months from the date of submission of trademark registration application for the said trademark in a foreign country for the first time, the applicant shall enjoy pre-emptive rights pursuant to the agreement executed between the said foreign country and China or the international treaty to which the said foreign country and China are participants, or pursuant to the principle of mutual acknowledgement of pre-emptive rights. An applicant asserting pre-emptive rights pursuant to the requirements of the preceding paragraph shall submit a written statement at the time of submission of trademark registration application, and submit the duplicate copy of the application documents for trademark registration for the first time within three months; failure to submit a written statement or failure to submit the duplicate copy of the application documents for trademark registration within the stipulated period shall be deemed as non-assertion of pre-emptive rights.
第二十六条 商标在中国政府主办的或者承认的国际展览会展出的商品上首次使用的，自该商品展出之日起六个月内，该商标的注册申请人可以享有优先权。 依照前款要求优先权的，应当在提出商标注册申请的时候提出书面声明，并且在三个月内提交展出其商品的展览会名称、在展出商品上使用该商标的证据、展出日期等证明文件；未提出书面声明或者逾期未提交证明文件的，视为未要求优先权。	**Article 26** Where a trademark is first used on commodities exhibited at an international exhibition organised or recognised by the Chinese Government, the applicant for trademark registration may enjoy pre-emptive rights within six months from the date of the exhibition of the said commodities. Where the applicant asserts pre-emptive rights
第二十七条 为申请商标注册所申报的事项和所提供的材料应当真实、准确、完整。	

第三章 商标注册的审查和核准	pursuant to the requirements of the preceding paragraph, it shall submit a written statement at the time of submission of trademark registration application, and submit proof documents for the name of exhibition of such commodities, proof of use of the said trademark on the commodities exhibited, date of exhibition, etc within three months; failure to submit a written statement or failure to submit proof documents within the stipulated period shall be deemed as non-assertion of pre-emptive rights.
第二十八条 对申请注册的商标，商标局应当自收到商标注册申请文件之日起九个月内审查完毕，符合本法有关规定的，予以初步审定公告。	**Article 27** Matters declared and materials submitted for trademark registration shall be true, accurate and complete.
第二十九条 在审查过程中，商标局认为商标注册申请内容需要说明或者修正的，可以要求申请人做出说明或者修正。申请人未做出说明或者修正的，不影响商标局做出审查决定。	**Chapter 3 Examination and Approval of Trademark Registration**
第三十条 申请注册的商标，凡不符合本法有关规定或者同他人在同一种商品或者类似商品上已经注册的或者初步审定的商标相同或者近似的，由商标局驳回申请，不予公告。	**Article 28** For trademark registration applications, the trademark bureau shall complete examination within nine months from the date of receipt of the trademark registration application documents, a preliminary validation gazette shall be made for applications which comply with the relevant provisions of this Law.
第三十一条 两个或者两个以上的商标注册申请人，在同一种商品或者类似商品上，以相同或者近似的商标申请注册的，初步审定并公告申请在先的商标；同一天申请的，初步审定并公告使用在先的商标，驳回其他人的申请，不予公告。	**Article 29** During the examination process, where the trademark bureau held that an explanation or correction is necessary for the contents of a trademark registration application, it may require the applicant to make the explanation or correction. The applicant's failure to make explanation or correction shall not affect the trademark bureau's making of an examination decision.
	Article 30 Trademark to be registered which does not comply

	with the relevant provisions of this Law or the subject matter trademark which is identical or similar to a trademark registered by others for the same type of commodities or similar commodities or a trademark preliminarily validated shall be thrown out by the trademark bureau and shall not be gazetted.
第三十二条 申请商标注册不得损害他人现有的在先权利，也不得以不正当手段抢先注册他人已经使用并有一定影响的商 标。	**Article 31** Where two or more applicants for trademark registration apply for registration of an identical or similar trademark for the same type of commodities or similar commodities, the earlier trademark registration shall be preliminarily validated and gazetted; where the trademark registration applications are submitted on the same day, the trademark which has been used earlier shall be preliminarily validated and gazetted, and the other applications shall be thrown out and shall not be gazetted.
第三十三条 对初步审定公告的商标，自公告之日起三个月内，在先权利人、利害关系人认为违反本法第十三条第二款和第三款、第十五条、第十六条第一款、第三十条、第三十一条、第三十二条规定的，或者任何人认为违反本法第四条、第十条、第十一条、第十二条、第十九条第四款规定的，可以向商标局提出异议。公告期满无异议的，予以核准注册，发给商标注册证，并予公告。	**Article 32** Trademark registration applications shall not harm existing prior rights of others, use of improper means to forestall registration of a trademark which is in use and has certain impact shall not be allowed.
第三十四条 对驳回申请、不予公告的商标，商标局应当书面通知商标注册申请人。商标注册申请人不服的，可以自收到通知之日起十五日内向商标评审委员会申请复审。商标评审委员会应当自收到申请之日起九个月内做出决定，并书面通知申请人。有特殊情况需要延长的，经国务院工商行政管理部门批准，可以延长三个月。当事人对商标评审委员会的决定不服的，可以自收到通知之日起三十日内向人民法院起诉。	**Article 33** A prior right holder or a stakeholder who holds that a preliminarily validated and gazetted trademark violates the provisions of the second and third paragraphs of Article 13, Article 15, the first paragraph of Article 16, Article 30, 31 or Article 32 of this Law, or any person who held that a preliminarily validated and gazetted trademark violates the provisions of Article 4, 10, 11, 12 or 19 of this Law may raise an objection to the trademark bureau within three months from the date of gazette. Where no objection is raised during the gazette period, the trademark shall be registered, a trademark registration certificate shall be issued

	and the registered trademark shall be gazetted. **Article 34** For applications which are thrown out and trademarks which are not gazetted, the trademark bureau shall notify the trademark registration applicants in writing. A trademark registration applicant who disagrees with the decision may apply to the trademark review and adjudication board for review within 15 days from the date of receipt of the notice. The trademark review and adjudication board shall make a decision within nine months from the date of receipt of the application, and notify the applicant in writing. Where there is a need for extension of time under special circumstances, upon approval by the administration for industry and commerce department of the State Council, a three-month extension may be allowed. A party concerned who disagrees with the decision of the trademark review and adjudication board may file a lawsuit with a People's Court within 30 days from the date of receipt of the notice.
第三十五条 对初步审定公告的商标提出异议的，商标局应当听取异议人和被异议人陈述事实和理由，经调查核实后，自公告期满之日起十二个月内做出是否准予注册的决定，并书面通知异议人和被异议人。有特殊情况需要延长的，经国务院工商行政管理部门批准，可以延长六个月。 商标局做出准予注册决定的，发给商标注册证，并予公告。异议人不服的，可以依照本法第四十四条、第四十五条的规定向商标评审委员会请求宣告该注册商标无效。 商标局做出不予注册决定，被异议人不服的，可以自收到通知之日起十五日内向商标评审委员会申请复审。商标评审委员会应当自收到申请之日起十二个月内做出复审决定，并书面通知异议人和被异议人。 有特殊情况需要延长的，经国务院工商行政管理部门批准，可以延长六个月。被异议人对商标评审委员会的决定不服的，可以自收到通知之日起三十日内向人民法院起诉。人民法院应当通知异议人作为第三人参加诉讼。 商标评审委员会在依照前款规定进行复审的过程中，所涉及的在先权利的确定必须以人民法院正在审理或者行政机关正在处理的另一案件的结果为依据的，可以中止审查。中止原因消除后，应当恢复审查程序。	**Article 35** In the case of an objection raised for a preliminarily validated and gazetted trademark, the trademark bureau shall heed the facts and reasons stated by the party which raises the objection and the party against whom the objection is raised, upon investigation and verification, the trademark bureau shall decide on registration or non-registration within 12 months from the date of expiry of the gazette period, and notify the party which raises the objection and the party against whom the objection is raised in writing. Where there is a need for extension of time under special circumstances, upon approval by the administration for industry and commerce department of the State Council, a six-month extension may be allowed. Where a decision for registration is made, the

	trademark bureau shall issue a trademark registration certificate to successful registrants and the registered trademark shall be gazetted. Where the party which raises the objection disagrees with the decision, it may apply to the trademark review and adjudication board pursuant to the provisions of Article 44 and Article 45 of this Law for invalidation of the said registered trademark. Where a decision for non-registration is made by the trademark bureau and the party against whom the objection is made disagrees with the decision, it may apply to the trademark review and adjudication board for review within 15 days from the date of receipt of the notice. The trademark review and adjudication board shall make a review decision within 12 months from the date of receipt of the application, and notify the party which raises the objection and the party against whom the objection is raised in writing. Where there is a need for extension of time under special circumstances, upon approval by the administration for industry and commerce department of the State Council, a six-month extension may be allowed. Where the party against whom the objection is made disagrees with the decision of the trademark review and adjudication board, it may file a lawsuit with a People's Court within 30 days from the date of receipt of the notice. The People's Court shall notify the party which raises the objection that it is listed as a third party in the lawsuit. Where the determination of prior rights involved in a review by the trademark review and adjudication board pursuant to the provisions of the preceding paragraph is to be based on the outcome of the trial of a lawsuit by a People's Court or the outcome of another case currently handled by the administrative authorities, examination may be suspended. The examination procedures shall be resumed upon elimination of the reason(s) for the suspension.
第三十六条 法定期限届满，当事人对商标局做出的驳回申请决定、不予注册决定不申请复审或者对商标评审委员会做出的复审决定不向人民法院起诉的，驳回申请决定、不予注册决定或者复审决定生效。 经审查异议不成立而准予注册的商标，商标注册申请人取得商标专用权的时间自初步审定公告三个月期满之日起计算。 自该商标公告期满之日起至准予注册决定做出前，对他人在同一种或者类似商品上使用与该商标相同或者近似的标志的行为不具有追溯力；但是，因该使用人的恶意给商标注册人造成的损失，应当给予赔偿。	

第三十七条 对商标注册申请和商标复审申请应当及时进行审查。 **第三十八条** 商标注册申请人或者注册人发现商标申请文件或者注册文件有明显错误的，可以申请更正。商标局依法在其职权范围内作出更正，并通知当事人。 前款所称更正错误不涉及商标申请文件或者注册文件的实质性内容。 **第四章 注册商标的续展、变更、转让和使用许可** **第三十九条** 注册商标的有效期为十年，自核准注册之日起计算。 **第四十条** 注册商标有效期满，需要继续使用的，商标注册人应当在期满前十二个月内按照规定办理续展手续；在此期间未能办理的，可以给予六个月的宽展期。每次续展注册的有效期为十年，自该商标上一届有效期满次日起计算。期满未办理续展手续的，注销其注册商标。 商标局应当对续展注册的商标予以公告。	**Article 36** Upon expiry of the statutory period, where a party concerned does not apply for review for a decision of the trademark bureau to throw out an application or a non-registration decision of the trademark bureau or does not file a lawsuit with a People's Court against a review decision of the trademark review and adjudication board, the decision to throw out an application, non-registration decision or review decision shall take effect. For a trademark which is registered after an objection is examined and found to be unjustifiable, the trademark registration applicant shall be deemed to have obtained exclusive rights to use the trademark on the date of expiry of a three-month period from the preliminary validation and gazette. During the period from the date of expiry of gazette period for the said trademark to the date of registration decision, the rights shall not apply retrospectively on the use of a mark identical or similar to the said trademark by others on the same type of commodities or similar commodities; however, where the malice use of the user causes the trademark registrant to suffer losses, such user(s) shall make compensation. **Article 37** Trademark registration applications and trademark review applications shall be promptly examined. **Article 38** A trademark registration applicant or a registrant who discovers an obvious error in its trademark application documents or registration documents may apply for correction to be made. The trademark bureau shall make correction within its terms of reference pursuant to the law and notify the party/parties) concerned. Correction of error referred to in the preceding

	paragraph shall not involve substantive contents of the trademark application documents or registration documents.
	Chapter 4 Renewal, Change, Transfer and Licensing of Registered Trademarks
	Article 39 A registered trademark shall be valid for 10 years, commencing from the date of registration.
第四十一条 注册商标需要变更注册人的名义、地址或者其他注册事项的，应当提出变更申请。	**Article 40** Upon expiry of the validity period of a registered trademark, where the trademark registrant intends to continue using the trademark, it shall complete renewal formalities pursuant to the provisions within the 12-month period before the expiry date; where renewal formalities are not completed within the stipulated period, a six-month extension may be allowed. The validity period of each renewal shall be 10 years, commencing from the date following expiry of the preceding validity period of the said trademark. Where renewal formalities are not completed upon expiry of the validity period, the registered trademark shall be cancelled. The trademark bureaux shall gazette renewed registered trademarks.
第四十二条 转让注册商标的，转让人和受让人应当签订转让协议，并共同向商标局提出申请。受让人应当保证使用该注册商标的商品质量。 转让注册商标的，商标注册人对其在同一种商品上注册的近似的商标，或者在类似商品上注册的相同或者近似的商标，应当一并转让。 对容易导致混淆或者有其他不良影响的转让，商标局不予核准，书面通知申请人并说明理由。 转让注册商标经核准后，予以公告。受让人自公告之日起享有商标专用权。	**Article 41** In the event of change of name or address of the registrant or change in any other registration matters of a registered trademark, an application for change shall be submitted.
第四十三条 商标注册人可以通过签订商标使用许可合同，许可他人使用其注册商标。许可人应当监督被许可人使用其注册商标的商品质量。被许可人应当保证使用该注册商标的商品质量。	**Article 42** In the case of transfer of registered trademark, the transferor and the transferee shall enter into a transfer agreement, and jointly submit an application to the trademark bureau. The transferee shall ensure the quality of the commodities on

经许可使用他人注册商标的，必须在使用该注册商标的商品上标明被许可人的名称和商品产地。 许可他人使用其注册商标的，许可人应当将其商标使用许可报商标局备案，由商标局公告。商标使用许可未经备案不得对抗善意第三人。	which the said registered trademark is used. In the case of transfer of registered trademark, any similar trademark registered by the trademark registrant for the same type of commodities, or any identical or similar trademark for similar commodities shall be transferred together. Transfers which may easily cause confusion or any other adverse impact shall not be approved by the trademark bureau, the applicant shall be notified in writing and the reason shall be stated. Upon approval of transfer of a registered trademark, the transfer shall be gazetted. The transferee shall enjoy exclusive rights to use trademark within effect from the date of gazette. **Article 43** A trademark registrant may execute a trademark licensing contract to license the use of its registered trademark to others. The licensor shall supervise the quality of commodities on which the said registered trademark is used by the licensee. The licensee shall ensure the quality of commodities on which the said registered trademark is used. For licensed use of a registered trademark, the name of the licensee and the place of origin of the commodities shall be stated on the commodities on which the said registered trademark is used. For licensed use of a registered trademark, the licensor shall file record of the licensing of the said trademark with the trademark bureau, and the licensing shall be gazetted by the trademark bureau. Non-filing of the licensing of a trademark shall not be contested against a good faith third party.
第五章 注册商标的无效宣告 **第四十四条** 已经注册的商标，违反本法第四条、第十条、第十一条、第十二条、第十九条第四款规定的，或者是以欺骗手段或者其他不正当手段取得注册的，由商标局宣告该注册商标无效；其他单位或者个人可以请求商标评审委员会宣告该注册商标无效。 商标局做出宣告注册商标无效的决定，应当书面通知当事人。当事人对商标局的决定不服的，可以自收到通知之日起十五日内向商标评审委员会申请复审。 商标评审委员会应当自收到申请之日起九个月内做出决定，并书面通知当事人。 有特殊情况需要延长的，经国务院工商行政管理部门批准，可以延长三个月。 当事人对商标评审委员会的决定不服的，可以自收到通知之日起三十日内向人民法院起诉。 其他单位或者个人请求商标评审委员会宣告注册商	**Chapter 5 Invalidation of Registered Trademarks** **Article 44** Where a registered trademark violates the

标无效的，商标评审委员会收到申请后，应当书面通知有关当事人，并限期提出答辩。 商标评审委员会应当自收到申请之日起九个月内做出维持注册商标或者宣告注册商标无效的裁定，并书面通知当事人。 有特殊情况需要延长的，经国务院工商行政管理部门批准，可以延长三个月。 当事人对商标评审委员会的裁定不服的，可以自收到通知之日起三十日内向人民法院起诉。人民法院应当通知商标裁定程序的对方当事人作为第三人参加诉讼。	provisions of Article 4, 10, 11 or 12 of this Law, or the fourth paragraph of Article 19 of this Law, or the registration is obtained by fraudulent means or other improper means, the registered trademark shall be invalidated by the trademark bureau; any other organisation or individual may request that the trademark review and adjudication board declares the said registered trademark invalid. Where the trademark bureau has made a decision on declaration of a registered trademark to be invalid, the party(ies) concerned shall be notified in writing. Where a party concerned disagrees with the decision of the trademark bureau, it may apply to the trademark review and adjudication board for review within 15 days from the date of receipt of the notice. The trademark review and adjudication board shall make a decision within nine months from the date of receipt of the application, and the party concerned shall be notified in writing. Where there is a need for extension of time under special circumstances, upon approval by the administration for industry and commerce department of the State Council, a three-month extension may be allowed. Where the party concerned disagrees with the decision of the trademark review and adjudication board, it may file a lawsuit with a People's Court within 30 days from the date of receipt of the notice.
第四十五条 已经注册的商标，违反本法第十三条第二款和第三款、第十五条、第十六条第一款、第三十条、第三十一条、第三十二条规定的，自商标注册之日起五年内，在先权利人或者利害关系人可以请求商标评审委员会宣告该注册商标无效。对恶意注册的，驰名商标所有人不受五年的时间限制。	Where any other organisation or individual requests that the trademark review and adjudication board declare a registered trademark invalid, the trademark review and adjudication board shall, upon receipt of the application, notify the relevant party(ies) concerned in writing, and enter a plea within the stipulated period. The trademark review and adjudication board shall

商标评审委员会收到宣告注册商标无效的申请后，应当书面通知有关当事人，并限期提出答辩。 商标评审委员会应当自收到申请之日起十二个月内做出维持注册商标或者宣告注册商标无效的裁定，并书面通知当事人。有特殊情况需要延长的，经国务院工商行政管理部门批准，可以延长六个月。 当事人对商标评审委员会的裁定不服的，可以自收到通知之日起三十日内向人民法院起诉。 人民法院应当通知商标裁定程序的对方当事人作为第三人参加诉讼。商标评审委员会在依照前款规定对无效宣告请求进行审查的过程中，所涉及的在先权利的确定必须以人民法院正在审理或者行政机关正在处理的另一案件的结果为依据的，可以中止审查。中止原因消除后，应当恢复审查程序。 **第四十六条** 法定期限届满，当事人对商标局宣告注册商标无效的决定不申请复审或者对商标评审委员会的复审决定、维持注册商标或者宣告注册商标无效的	make a ruling on upholding or invalidation of the registered trademark within nine months from the date of receipt of the application, and notify the party concerned in writing. Where there is a need for extension of time under special circumstances, upon approval by the administration for industry and commerce department of the State Council, a three-month extension may be allowed. Where the party concerned disagrees with the ruling of the trademark review and adjudication board, it may file a lawsuit with a People's Court within 30 days from the date of receipt of the notice. The People's Court shall notify the counterparty in the trademark adjudication procedures that it is listed as a third party in the lawsuit. **Article 45** Where a registered trademark violates the provisions of the second and third paragraphs of Article 13, Article 15, the first paragraph of Article 16, Article 30, Article 31 or Article 32 of this Law, a prior right holder or a stakeholder may, within five years from the date of trademark registration, request that the trademark review and adjudication board declares the said registered trademark invalid. For malicious registrations, holders of well-known trademarks shall not be subject to the five-year restriction. The trademark review and adjudication board shall, upon receipt of an application for invalidation of registered trademark, notify the relevant party(ies) concerned in writing, and enter a plea within the stipulated period. The trademark review and adjudication board shall make a ruling on upholding or invalidation of registered trademark within 12 months from the date of receipt of the application, and notify the party(ies) concerned in writing. Where there is a need for extension of time under special circumstances, upon approval by the administration for industry and commerce department of the State Council, a six-month

裁定不向人民法院起诉的，商标局的决定或者商标评审委员会的复审决定、裁定生效。	extension may be allowed. Where a party concerned disagrees with the ruling of the trademark review and adjudication board, it may file a lawsuit with a People's Court within 30 days from the date of receipt of the notice. The People's Court shall notify the counterparty in the trademark adjudication procedures that it is listed as a third party in the lawsuit.
第四十七条 依照本法第四十四条、第四十五条的规定宣告无效的注册商标，由商标局予以公告，该注册商标专用权视为自始即不存在。 宣告注册商标无效的决定或者裁定，对宣告无效前人民法院做出并已执行的商标侵权案件的判决、裁定、调解书和工商行政管理部门做出并已执行的商标侵权案件的处理决定以及已经履行的商标转让或者使用许可合同不具有追溯力。但是，因商标注册人的恶意给他人造成的损失，应当给予赔偿。 依照前款规定不返还商标侵权赔偿金、商标转让费、商标使用费，明显违反公平原则的，应当全部或者部分返还。	During the examination of a request for invalidation by the trademark review and adjudication board pursuant to the provisions of the preceding paragraph, where the determination of prior rights involved is to be based on the outcome of the trial of a lawsuit by a People's Court or the outcome of another case currently handled by the administrative authorities, examination may be suspended. The examination procedures shall be resumed upon elimination of the reason(s) for the suspension. **Article 46** Upon expiry of the statutory period, where a party concerned does not apply for a review in respect of the decision of the trademark bureau on invalidation of a registered trademark or does not file a lawsuit with a People's Court against the review decision of the trademark review and adjudication board or the ruling on upholding or invalidation of registered trademark , the decision of the trademark bureau or the review decision or ruling of the trademark review and adjudication board shall take effect.
第六章 商标使用的管理	**Article 47** Registered trademarks invalidated pursuant to the provisions of Article 44 or Article 45 of this Law shall be gazetted by the trademark bureau, the exclusive rights to use the said registered trademark shall be deemed non-existent from the beginning.
第四十八条 本法所称商标的使用，是指将商标用于商	A decision or ruling on invalidation of registered trademark shall not apply retrospectively on a

品、商品包装或者容器以及商品交易文书上，或者将商标用于广告宣传、展览以及其他商业活动中，用于识别商品来源的行 为。 **第四十九条** 商标注册人在使用注册商标的过程中，自行改变注册商标、注册人名义、地址或者其他注册事项的，由地方工商行政管理部门责令限期改正；期满不改正的，由商标局撤销其注册商标。 注册商标成为其核定使用的商品的通用名称或者没有正当理由连续三年不使用的，任何单位或者个人可以向商标局申请撤销该注册商标。 商标局应当自收到申请之日起九个月内做出决定。有特殊情况需要延长的，经国务院工商行政管理部门批准，可以延长三个月。 **第五十条** 注册商标被撤销、被宣告无效或者期满不再续展的，自撤销、宣告无效或者注销之日起一年内，商标局对与该商标相同或者近似的商标注册申请，不予核准。	judgment or ruling for a trademark infringement lawsuit passed by a People's Court prior to the invalidation which has been implemented, a mediation letter, a handling decision on a trademark infringement case made by the administration for industry and commerce which has been implemented or a trademark transfer or licensing contract which has been performed. However, where the malice of the trademark registrant causes others to suffer losses, the trademark registrant shall make compensation. Where non-refund of trademark infringement compensation, trademark transfer fee or trademark licensing fee pursuant to the provisions of the preceding paragraph is evidently in violation of the principle of fairness, full or partial amount shall be refunded. **Chapter 6 Administration of Trademark Use** **Article 48** Trademark use referred to in this Law shall mean use of a trademark on commodities, commodity packaging or containers and commercial transaction documents, or use of a trademark in advertisement and promotion, exhibition and other commercial activities, for identifying the source of commodities. **Article 49** Trademark registrants who make arbitrary changes to a registered trademark, the registrant's name or address or any other registration matter in the course of use of a registered trademark shall be ordered by the local administration for industry and commerce to make correction within a stipulated period; where correction is not made within the stipulated period, the registered trademark shall be revoked by the trademark bureau. Where a registered trademark becomes a generic

第五十一条 违反本法第六条规定的，由地方工商行政管理部门责令限期申请注册，违法经营额五万元以上的，可以处违法经营额百分之二十以下的罚款，没有违法经营额或者违法经营额不足五万元的，可以处一万元以下的罚款。 **第五十二条** 将未注册商标冒充注册商标使用的，或者使用未注册商标违反本法第十条规定的，由地方工商行政管理部门予以制止，限期改正，并可以予以通报，违法经营额五万元以上的，可以处违法经营额百分之二十以下的罚款，没有违法经营额或者违法经营额不足五万元的，可以处一万元以下的罚款。 **第五十三条** 违反本法第十四条第五款规定的，由地方工商行政管理部门责令改正，处十万元罚款。 **第五十四条** 对商标局撤销或者不予撤销注册商标的决定，当事人不服的，可以自收到通知之日起十五日内向商标评审委员会申请复审。商标评审委员会应当自收到申请之日起九个月内做出决定，并书面通知当事人。 有特殊情况需要延长的，经国务院工商行政管理部门	name of the commodities for which it is approved or a registered trademark has not been used for three years consecutively without a proper reason, any organisation or individual may apply to the trademark bureau for revocation of the said registered trademark. The trademark bureau shall make a decision within nine months from the date of receipt of the application. Where there is a need for extension of time under special circumstances, upon approval by the administration for industry and commerce department of the State Council, a three-month extension may be allowed. **Article 50** Where a registered trademark is revoked, invalidated or not renewed upon expiry of its validity period, the trademark bureau shall, within one year from the date of revocation, invalidation or cancellation, not approve trademark registration applications for trademarks identical or similar to the said trademark. **Article 51** Persons who violate the provisions of Article 6 of this Law shall be ordered by the local administration for industry and commerce to submit registration application within a stipulated period, a fine of not more than 20% of the illegal turnover may be imposed on persons whose illegal turnover is RMB50,000 or more; where there is no illegal turnover or the illegal turnover is below RMB50,000, a fine of not more than RMB10,000 may be imposed. **Article 52** Persons who use a unregistered trademark to pose off as a registered trademark or whose use of a unregistered trademark violates the provisions of Article 10 of this Law shall be curbed by the local administration for industry and commerce and ordered to make correction within a stipulated

批准，可以延长三个月。 当事人对商标评审委员会的决定不服的，可以自收到通知之日起三十日内向人民法院起诉。	period, and the punishment decision may be circulated, a fine of not more than 20% of the illegal turnover may be imposed on persons whose illegal turnover is RMB50,000 or more; where there is no illegal turnover or the illegal turnover is below RMB50,000, a fine of not more than RMB10,000 may be imposed. **Article 53** Persons who violate the provisions of the fifth paragraph of Article 14 of this Law shall be ordered by the local administration for industry and commerce to make correction and be subject to a fine of RMB100,000.
第五十五条 法定期限届满，当事人对商标局做出的撤销注册商标的决定不申请复审或者对商标评审委员会做出的复审决定不向人民法院起诉的，撤销注册商标的决定、复审决定生效。 被撤销的注册商标，由商标局予以公告，该注册商标专用权自公告之日起终止。 **第七章 注册商标专用权的保护** **第五十六条** 注册商标的专用权，以核准注册的商标和核定使用的商品为限。 **第五十七条** 有下列行为之一的，均属侵犯注册商标专用权： (一)未经商标注册人的许可，在同一种商品上使用与	**Article 54** Where a party concerned disagrees with the decision on revocation or non-revocation of registered trademark by the trademark bureau, it may apply to the trademark review and adjudication board for review within 15 days from the date of receipt of the notice. The trademark review and adjudication board shall make a decision within nine months from the date of receipt of the application, and notify the party / parties concerned in writing. Where there is a need for extension of time under special circumstances, upon approval by the administration for industry and commerce department of the State Council, a three-month extension may be allowed. Where a party concerned disagrees with the decision of the trademark review and adjudication board, it may file a lawsuit with a People's Court within 30 days from the date of receipt of the notice. **Article 55** Upon expiry of the statutory period, where a party concerned does not apply for a review in respect of the decision of the trademark bureau on revocation of a registered trademark or does not file a lawsuit with a People's Court against the review decision of

其注册商标相同的商标的； (二)未经商标注册人的许可，在同一种商品上使用与其注册商标近似的商标，或者在类似商品上使用与其注册商标相同或者近似的商标，容易导致混淆的； (三)销售侵犯注册商标专用权的商品的； (四)伪造、擅自制造他人注册商标标识或者销售伪造、擅自制造的注册商标标识的； (五)未经商标注册人同意，更换其注册商标并将该更换商标的商品又投入市场的； (六)故意为侵犯他人商标专用权行为提供便利条件，帮助他人实施侵犯商标专用权行为的； (七)给他人的注册商标专用权造成其他损害的。	the trademark review and adjudication board, the decision on revocation of registered trademark or the review decision shall take effect. Revoked registered trademarks shall be gazetted by the trademark bureau, the exclusive rights to use registered trademarks shall terminate on the date of gazette. **Chapter 7 Protection of Exclusive Rights to Use Registered Trademarks** **Article 56** Exclusive rights to use a registered trademark shall be limited to the approved registered trademark and the commodities for which the trademark is approved for use.
第五十八条 将他人注册商标、未注册的驰名商标作为企业名称中的字号使用，误导公众，构成不正当竞争行为的，依照《中华人民共和国反不正当竞争法》处理。 **第五十九条** 注册商标中含有的本商品的通用名称、图形、型号，或者直接表示商品的质量、主要原料、功能、用途、重量、数量及其他特点，或者含有的地名，注册商标专用权人无权禁止他人正当使用。 三维标志注册商标中含有的商品自身的性质产生的	**Article 57** Any of the following acts shall be deemed as infringement of exclusive rights to use registered trademarks: (1) use of a trademark identical to a registered trademark on the same type of commodities without licensing by the trademark registrant; (2) use of a trademark similar to a registered trademark on the same type of commodities without licensing by the trademark registrant, or use of a trademark identical or similar to the registered trademark on similar commodities which easily causes confusion; (3) sale of commodities which infringe upon exclusive rights to use registered trademarks; (4) forgery or unauthorised manufacturing of labels of other's registered trademark or sale of forged or unauthorised labels of other's registered trademark; (5) change of a registered trademark without the consent of the trademark registrant, and sale of commodities bearing the changed trademark in the market;

形状、为获得技术效果而需有的商品形状或者使商品具有实质性价值的形状，注册商标专用权人无权禁止他人正当使用。 商标注册人申请商标注册前，他人已经在同一种商品或者类似商品上先于商标注册人使用与注册商标相同或者近似并有一定影响的商标的，注册商标专用权人无权禁止该使用人在原使用范围内继续使用该商标，但可以要求其附加适当区别标识。	(6) intentionally facilitating infringement of other's exclusive rights to use trademarks, assisting others in implementation of infringement of exclusive rights to use trademarks; or (7) causing harm to other's exclusive rights to use registered trademarks.
	Article 58 Use of other's registered trademark or an unregistered well-known trademark as an enterprise name to mislead the public which constitutes unfair competition shall be dealt with pursuant to the Anti-unfair Competition Law of the People's Republic of China.
第六十条 有本法第五十七条所列侵犯注册商标专用权行为之一，引起纠纷的，由当事人协商解决；不愿协商或者协商不成的，商标注册人或者利害关系人可以向人民法院起诉，也可以请求工商行政管理部门处理。 工商行政管理部门处理时，认定侵权行为成立的，责令立即停止侵权行为，没收、销毁侵权商品和主要用于制造侵权商品、伪造注册商标标识的工具，违法经营额五万元以上的，可以处违法经营额五倍以下的罚款，没有违法经营额或者违法经营额不足五万元的，可以处二十五万元以下的罚款。 对五年内实施两次以上商标侵权行为或者有其他严重情节的，应当从重处罚。	**Article 59** In the case of a generic name, figure or model number of commodities in a registered trademark or direct expression of the quality, key ingredients, functions, purposes, weight, quantity and other characteristics of commodities in a registered name or a geographical name in a registered trademark, the holder of exclusive rights to use trademarks shall have no right to prohibit proper use by others. In the case of a shape arising from the characteristics of the commodities in a registered three-dimensional trademark or a shape of commodities required to obtain technical results in a registered three-dimensional trademark or a shape which gives the commodities substantial value in a registered three-dimensional trademark, the holder of exclusive rights to use trademarks shall have no right to prohibit proper use by others. Prior to a trademark registration application by a trademark registrant, where another party has used a trademark which is identical or similar to the registered trademark and has a certain reputation on the same type of commodities or similar

销售不知道是侵犯注册商标专用权的商品，能证明该商品是自己合法取得并说明提供者的，由工商行政管理部门责令停止销售。 对侵犯商标专用权的赔偿数额的争议，当事人可以请求进行处理的工商行政管理部门调解，也可以依照《中华人民共和国民事诉讼法》向人民法院起诉。 经工商行政管理部门调解，当事人未达成协议或者调解书生效后不履行的，当事人可以依照《中华人民共和国民事诉讼法》向人民法院起诉。 **第六十一条** 对侵犯注册商标专用权的行为，工商行政管理部门有权依法查处；涉嫌犯罪的，应当及时移送司法机关依法处理。	commodities before the trademark registrant, the holder of exclusive rights to use registered trademarks shall have no right to prohibit the said user to continue use of the said trademark within the original scope of use, but may request that the user to insert appropriate additional distinguishing mark(s). **Article 60** In the event of a dispute arising from any of the acts of infringement of exclusive rights to use registered trademarks mentioned in Article 57 of this Law, the parties concerned shall negotiate for resolution; where the parties concerned are unwilling to negotiate or where negotiation is unsuccessful, the trademark registrant or a stakeholder may file a lawsuit with a People's Court or request that the administration for industry and commerce handles the dispute. Where the administration for industry and commerce handling the dispute held that there is infringement, the infringor shall be ordered to stop the infringing act, the infringing commodities and the tools mainly used for manufacturing of the infringing commodities and forgery of registered trademark labels shall be confiscated and destroyed; for persons whose illegal turnover is RMB50,000 or more, a fine of not more than five times the amount of illegal turnover may be imposed; where there is no illegal turnover or the illegal turnover is below RMB50,000, a fine of not more than RMB250,000 may be imposed. Persons who have committed trademark infringement on two or more occasions within five years or persons who have committed other serious offences shall be subject to severe punishment. In the case of persons who engage in sale of commodities which infringe upon exclusive rights to use registered trademarks without knowledge of the infringement, where it can be proven that the commodities are

	obtained legitimately and the supplier of the said commodities can be stated, the offender shall be ordered by the administration for industry and commerce to stop selling the infringing commodities. In the case of a dispute over the compensation amount for infringement of exclusive rights to use trademarks, the party concerned may request for mediation by the administration for industry and commerce handling the matter, and may file a lawsuit with a People's Court pursuant to the Civil Procedure Law of the People's Republic of China. Upon mediation by the administration for industry and commerce, where the parties concerned are unable to conclude an agreement or the mediation letter which has taken effect is not performed, the parties concerned may file a lawsuit with a People's Court pursuant to the Civil Procedure Law of the People's Republic of China. **Article 61** The administration for industry and commerce shall have the right to investigate infringement of exclusive rights to use registered trademarks pursuant to the law; where the case constitutes a criminal offence, the case shall be promptly forwarded to the judicial authorities for handling pursuant to the law.
第六十二条 县级以上工商行政管理部门根据已经取得的违法嫌疑证据或者举报，对涉嫌侵犯他人注册商标专用权的行为进行查处时，可以行使下列职权： (一)询问有关当事人，调查与侵犯他人注册商标专用权有关的情况； (二)查阅、复制当事人与侵权活动有关的合同、发票、账簿以及其他有关资料； (三)对当事人涉嫌从事侵犯他人注册商标专用权活动的场所实施现场检查； (四)检查与侵权活动有关的物品；对有证据证明是侵犯他人注册商标专用权的物品，可以查封或者扣押。 工商行政管理部门依法行使前款规定的职权时，当事人应当予以协助、配合，不得拒绝、阻挠。 在查处商标侵权案件过程中，对商标权属存在争议或者权利人同时向人民法院提起商标侵权诉讼的，工商行政管理部门可以中止案件的查处。中止原因消除后，应当恢复或者终结案件查处程序。	**Article 62** Administration for industry and commerce of county level and above may exercise the following powers in the investigation of an alleged infringement of other's exclusive rights to use registered trademarks based on the evidence or reporting of an illegal act or a suspect: (1) interview the relevant parties involved, investigate into information pertaining to infringement of other's exclusive rights to use registered trademarks;
第六十三条 侵犯商标专用权的赔偿数额，按照权利人	(2) read or make copies of contracts, invoices,

因被侵权所受到的实际损失确定；实际损失难以确定的，可以按照侵权人因侵权所获得的利益确定；权利人的损失或者侵权人获得的利益难以确定的，参照该商标许可使用费的倍数合理确定。对恶意侵犯商标专用权，情节严重的，可以在按照上述方法确定数额的一倍以上五倍以下确定赔偿数额。赔偿数额应当包括权利人为制止侵权行为所支付的合理开支。 人民法院为确定赔偿数额，在权利人已经尽力举证，而与侵权行为相关的账簿、资料主要由侵权人掌握的情况下，可以责令侵权人提供与侵权行为相关的账簿、资料；侵权人不提供或者提供虚假的账簿、资料的，人民法院可以参考权利人的主张和提供的证据判定赔偿数额。 权利人因被侵权所受到的实际损失、侵权人因侵权所获得的利益、注册商标许可使用费难以确定的，由人民法院根据侵权行为的情节判决给予五百万元以下的赔偿。 人民法院审理商标纠纷案件，应权利人请求，对属于假冒注册商标的商品，除特殊情况外，责令销毁；对主要用于制造假冒注册商标的商品的材料、工具，责令销毁，且不予补偿；或者在特殊情况下，责令禁止前述材料、工具进入商业渠道，且不予补偿。 假冒注册商标的商品不得在仅去除假冒注册商标后进入商业渠道。 **第六十四条** 注册商标专用权人请求赔偿，被控侵权人以注册商标专用权人未使用注册商标提出抗辩的，人民法院可以要求注册商标专用权人提供此前三年内实际使用该注册商标的证据。注册商标专用权人不能	accounts books and other relevant materials of the parties concerned which relate to the infringement activities; (3) conduct onsite inspection of the premises of the parties involved where the infringement of other's exclusive rights to use registered trademarks is allegedly committed; or (4) inspect articles which relate to the infringement activities; may seize or confiscate articles for which there is evidence to prove infringement of other's exclusive rights to use registered trademarks. When the administration for industry and commerce exercises the powers stipulated in the preceding paragraph pursuant to the law, the parties concerned shall assist or render cooperation, and shall not refuse or hinder. In the course of investigation of a trademark infringement case, where there is dispute over the ownership of trademark rights or the right holder has simultaneously filed a trademark infringement lawsuit with a People's Court, the administration for industry and commerce may suspend investigation of the case. Upon elimination of the reason(s) for suspension, the investigation procedures shall be resumed or terminated. **Article 63** The compensation amount for infringement of exclusive rights to use trademarks shall be determined in accordance with the actual losses suffered by the right holder due to the infringement; where it is difficult to determine the actual losses, the compensation amount may be determined in accordance with the gains derived by the infringor from the infringement; where it is difficult to determine the losses of the right holder or the gains derived by the infringement, the compensation amount shall be determined reasonably with reference to the multiples of the licensing fee of the said trademark. For malicious infringement of exclusive rights to use trademarks, in serious

证明此前三年内实际使用过该注册商标，也不能证明因侵权行为受到其他损失的，被控侵权人不承担赔偿责任。 销售不知道是侵犯注册商标专用权的商品，能证明该商品是自己合法取得并说明提供者的，不承担赔偿责任 **第六十五条** 商标注册人或者利害关系人有证据证明他人正在实施或者即将实施侵犯其注册商标专用权的行为，如不及时制止将会使其合法权益受到难以弥补的损害的，可以依法在起诉前向人民法院申请采取责令停止有关行为和财产保全的措施。 **第六十六条** 为制止侵权行为，在证据可能灭失或者以后难以取得的情况下，商标注册人或者利害关系人可以依法在起诉前向人民法院申请保全证据。 **第六十七条** 未经商标注册人许可，在同一种商品上使用与其注册商标相同的商标，构成犯罪的，除赔偿被侵权人的损失外，依法追究刑事责任。 伪造、擅自制造他人注册商标标识或者销售伪造、擅自制造的注册商标标识，构成犯罪的，除赔偿被侵权人的损失外，依法追究刑事责任。 销售明知是假冒注册商标的商品，构成犯罪的，除赔偿被侵权人的损失外，依法追究刑事责任。	cases, the compensation amount shall be determined in accordance with the aforesaid method based on one to five times of the determined amount. The compensation amount shall include reasonable expenses incurred by the right holder to curb the infringement. In the determination of compensation amount by the People's Court, where the right holder has provided proof to its best effort, and the accounts books and materials relating to the infringement are held by the infringor, the People's Court may order the infringer to provide accounts books and materials relating to the infringement; where the infringer does not provide accounts books and materials or where the accounts books and materials provided are false, the People's Court may determine the compensation amount with reference to the assertion of the right holder and the evidence provided. Where it is difficult to determine the actual losses suffered by the right holder due to the infringement or the gains derived by the infringor from the infringement or the licensing fee of the registered trademark, the People's Court shall rule on a compensation amount of not more than RMB 5 million based on the extent of the infringement. The People's Court hearing a trademark-related dispute shall, as requested by the right holder, order to destroy the commodities bearing a counterfeited registered trademark, with the exception of special circumstances; for the materials and tools mainly used to manufacture the commodities bearing a counterfeited registered trademark, the People's Court shall order to destroy them, without any compensation; or in particular cases, the People's Court shall prohibit the said materials and tools from entering commercial channels, without any compensation. The commodities bearing a counterfeited registered trademark shall not enter commercial channels even though they do not bear the said trademark

第六十八条 商标代理机构有下列行为之一的，由工商行政管理部门责令限期改正，给予警告，处一万元以上十万元以下的罚款；对直接负责的主管人员和其他直接责任人员给予警告，处五千元以上五万元以下的罚款；构成犯罪的，依法追究刑事责任： （一）办理商标事宜过程中，伪造、变造或者使用伪造、变造的法律文件、印章、签名的； （二）以诋毁其他商标代理机构等手段招徕商标代理业务或者以其他不正当手段扰乱商标代理市场秩序的； （三）违反本法第四条、第十九条第三款和第四款规定的； 商标代理机构有前款规定行为的，由工商行政管理部门记入信用档案；情节严重的，商标局、商标评审委员会并可以决定停止受理其办理商标代理业务，予以公告。 商标代理机构违反诚实信用原则，侵害委托人合法利益的，应当依法承担民事责任，并由商标代理行业组织按照章程规定予以惩戒。 对恶意申请商标注册的，根据情节给予警告、罚款等行政处罚；对恶意提起商标诉讼的，由人民法院依法给予处罚。 **第六十九条** 从事商标注册、管理和复审工作的国家机关工作人员必须秉公执法，廉洁自律，忠于职守，文明服务。 商标局、商标评审委员会以及从事商标注册、管理和复审工作的国家机关工作人员不得从事商标代理业	any longer. **Article 64** Where a holder of exclusive rights to use registered trademarks seeks compensation, the alleged infringor pleaded that the holder of exclusive rights to use registered trademarks has not used the registered trademark, the People's Court may require the holder of exclusive rights to use registered trademarks to provide evidence of actual use of the said registered trademark during the preceding three-year period. Where the holder of exclusive rights to use registered trademark cannot prove that it has actually used the said registered trademarks during the preceding three-year period, and cannot prove that it has suffered other losses due to the infringement, the alleged infringor shall not bear compensation liability. Where a person who engages in sale of commodities which infringe upon exclusive rights to use registered trademarks without knowledge of the infringement can prove that the said commodities are obtained legitimately and the supplier of the said commodities can be stated, it shall not bear compensation liability. **Article 65** Where a trademark registrant or a stakeholder has evidence to prove that others are implementing or are going to implement infringement of its exclusive rights to use registered trademarks, and that it will suffer irreparable damage of its legitimate interests if the infringement is not stopped promptly, it may, prior to the lawsuit, apply to the People's Court pursuant to the law for an order to stop the relevant act(s) and for property preservation measures. **Article 66** For the purpose of curbing an infringement, where the evidence may be lost or destroyed or difficult to obtain in the future, a trademark registrant or a stakeholder may, prior to the lawsuit, apply to the

务和商品生产经营活动。 **第七十条** 工商行政管理部门应当建立健全内部监督制度，对负责商标注册、管理和复审工作的国家机关工作人员执行法律、行政法规和遵守纪律的情况，进行监督检查。 **第七十一条** 从事商标注册、管理和复审工作的国家机关工作人员玩忽职守、滥用职权、徇私舞弊，违法办理商标注册、管理和复审事项，收受当事人财物，牟取不正当利益，构成犯罪的，依法追究刑事责任；尚不构成犯罪的，依法给予处分。 **第八章 附则** **第七十二条** 申请商标注册和办理其他商标事宜的，应当缴纳费用，具体收费标准另定。 **第七十三条** 本法自 1983 年 3 月 1 日起施行。1963 年 4 月 10 日国务院公布的《商标管理条例》同时废止；其他有关商标管理的规定，凡与本法抵触的，同时失效。本法施行前已经注册的商标继续有效。	People's Court for preservation of evidence pursuant to the law. **Article 67** Where the use of a trademark identical to a registered trademark on the same type of commodities without licensing by the trademark registrant constitutes a criminal offence, in addition to compensation of the losses of the infringed party, criminal liability shall be pursued in accordance with the law. Where the forgery or unauthorised manufacturing of other's registered trademark labels or sale of forged or unauthorised registered trademark labels constitutes a criminal offence, in addition to compensation of the losses of the infringed party, criminal liability shall be pursued in accordance with the law. Where the sale of commodities bearing a counterfeited registered trademark when the seller is aware of the counterfeit constitutes a criminal offence, in addition to compensation of the losses of the infringed party, criminal liability shall be pursued in accordance with the law. **Article 68** Trademark agencies which commit any of the following acts shall be ordered by the administration for industry and commerce to make correction within a stipulated period and be subject to a warning and a fine ranging from RMB10,000 to RMB100,000; the person(s)-in-charge who is/are directly responsible and other directly accountable personnel shall be subject to a warning and a fine ranging from RMB5,000 to RMB50,000; where the case constitutes a criminal offence, criminal liability shall be pursued in accordance with the law: (1) forgery or alteration of legal documents, seals or signatures or use of forged or altered legal documents, seals or signatures in the course of handling trademark matters;

	(2) solicitation of trademark agency business by defaming other trademark agencies, etc or use of improper means to disrupt the order of the trademark agency market; or (3) violation of the provisions of Article 4 of this Law or the third and fourth paragraphs of Article 19 of this Law. Trademark agencies which commit any of the acts stipulated in the preceding paragraph shall be recorded in the trustworthiness files of the administration for industry and commerce; in serious cases, the trademark bureau and the trademark review and adjudication board may decide to suspend acceptance of applications submitted by them as a trademark agent, and an announcement shall be made. Trademark agencies which violate the principles of honesty and trustworthiness and harm the legitimate interests of an entrusting party shall bear civil liability pursuant to the law, and shall be punished by the trademark agency industry organisation pursuant to the provisions of its articles of association. Whoever maliciously applies for trademark registration shall be subject to subject to a warning, a fine or any other administrative punishments, as the case may be; and whoever maliciously lodges a trademark lawsuit shall be penalized by the People's Court according to law. **Article 69** State agency officers engaging in trademark registration, administration and review shall carry out law enforcement impartially, exercise probity and self-discipline, act with dedication, and provide services in a civilised manner. Trademark bureaux and the trademark review and adjudication board and State agency officers engaging in trademark registration, administration and review shall not engage in trademark agency business and manufacturing and business activities

	of commodities. **Article 70** Administration for industry and commerce shall establish and improve upon an internal supervision system, carry out supervision and inspection of implementation of laws, administrative regulations and discipline by State agency officers responsible for trademark registration, administration and review. **Article 71** In the case of State agency officers engaging in trademark registration, administration and review guilty of dereliction of duty, abusing official powers or corruption, handling trademark registration, administration and review matters in an illegal manner, receiving monies from a party concerned, or seeking improper gains, where the case constitutes a criminal offence, criminal liability shall be pursued in accordance with the law; where the case does not constitute a criminal offence, punishment shall be imposed pursuant to the law. **Chapter 8 Supplementary Provisions** **Article 72** Fees shall be paid for trademark registration applications and handling of other trademark matters, detailed fee rates shall be stipulated separately. **Article 73** This Law shall be effective 1 March 1983. The Administrative Regulations on Trademarks promulgated by the State Council on 10 October 1963 shall be repealed simultaneously; where there is any discrepancy between this Law and other provisions on trademark administration, such other provisions shall become void simultaneously. Trademarks registered prior to implementation of this Law shall continue to be valid.

The manufacturer's authorised representative in the EU is Springer Nature Customer Service Centre GmbH, Europaplatz 3, 69115 Heidelberg, Germany. If you have any concerns regarding our products, please contact ProductSafety@springernature.com

Printed and bound by CPI Group (UK) Ltd, Croydon, CR0 4YY
25/09/2026
02222903-0009